Sports Illustrated

M V P

MOST VALUABLE PUZZLES

WELCOME

SPORTS ILLUSTRATED'S first venture into the world of puzzle books features old faves such as crosswords and picture puzzles, and also a new kind of puzzle called a cross stat that is tailor-made for sports trivia fanatics. Just turn the page and . . . let the games begin!

CROSSWORDS THAT TACKLE SPORTS SUPERSTARS

15-Across

Star with Stripes

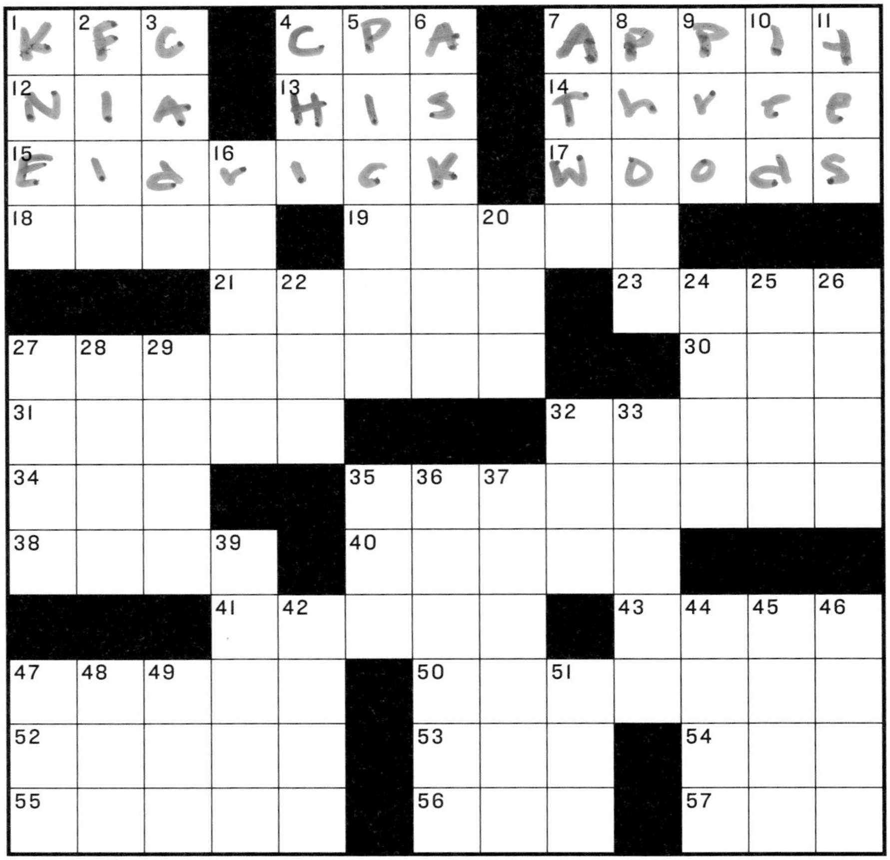

ACROSS

1 Chain with a "wing flapping" Super Bowl XLIII promotion
4 Tax season V.I.P.
7 Make a college try?
12 Actress Long of *Big Momma's House*
13 ___ nobs (cribbage score)
14 Number of U.S. Amateur Championships won by Tiger
15 Tiger's first name
17 Tiger's last name
18 Ernie "The Big ___" Els
19 Used ___ wedge (kicked one's golfball)
21 Ann ___, home of the Wolverines
23 Is ___ (plays below varsity)
27 Where Tiger was dubbed Urkel by his teammates
30 Extra-wide shoe size
31 Ticket-sale spot
32 Seat wiper
34 Startled cry
35 Sunday wear for Tiger
38 Singer Brickell or Adams
40 "...was stirring, not ___ mouse"
41 U.S. Army rank for Tiger's dad
43 The Fosbury ___
47 Tiger's Kiwi caddie
50 Tiger's mother
52 Green gimme
53 Many athletes have a big one
54 Golfers Sneed and Fiori
55 Practical joke
56 It might end 6-4 or 7-5
57 Mil. draft org.

DOWN

1 Where Tiger had 2008 surgery
2 Nike rival
3 Scoundrels
4 The Fire, on a scoreboard
5 Street that goes downhill?
6 Request, as a ruling
7 Shot ___ on (birdied a 205-yard hole)
8 ___ finish
9 PGA Tour player
10 Was ahead of
11 Yankees TV network
16 Pitcher Nolan and others
20 Luggage letters at O'Hare
22 Where the 'Skins once played
24 Radar O'Reilly's favorite soda
25 Act the boobird
26 Type of skateboarding ramp
27 ___-ball (arcade game)
28 Headed for sudden death
29 Golfer Isao
32 *Top Gun* org.
33 Clubhead holder
35 Type of room for games
36 Brings to mind
37 Torrential tournament stopper
39 Hayes who was the No. 1 NBA pick in 1968
42 6.2 mile race
44 Fairway positions
45 Vegas sets them
46 Typical call on 3rd and long
47 "The Racer's Edge"
48 1909 Indy track coating
49 Emissions org.
51 Stadium surrounder, often

Answer on page 136

The Rundown

BIRTHDAY Dec. 30, 1975

BIRTHPLACE Cypress, Calif.

FUN FACT In 1998, he became the eighth "permanent endorser" for Wheaties, joining Bob Richards ('58), Bruce Jenner ('77), Mary Lou Retton ('84), Pete Rose ('85), Walter Payton ('86), Chris Evert ('87) and Michael Jordan ('88).

STATS ENTERTAINMENT In '91 he became the youngest golfer to win the U.S. Junior Amateur, which he won a record three straight times. In '94, he became the youngest to win the U.S. Amateur, which he also won a record three straight times.

HE SAID IT In 2005: "If money titles meant anything, I'd play more tournaments. The only thing that means a lot to me is winning. If I have more wins than anybody else and win more majors than anybody else in the same year, then it's been a good year."

FROM THE SI VAULT "When the boy was seven, his parents installed the psychological armor. If he had a full wedge shot, the father would stand 15 feet in front of him and say, "I'm a tree." And the kid would have to hit over him. The father would jingle his change before the boy's bunker shots. Pump the brake on the cart on the boy's mid-irons. Rip the Velcro on his glove over a three-footer. What his dad tried to do, whenever possible, was cheat, distract, harass and annoy him. It was not good enough that by age two the boy could look at a grown man's swing and understand it ("Look, Daddy," he would say, "that man has a reverse pivot!"); that by three he was beating 10-year-olds; that by five he was signing autographs (because he couldn't write script, he printed his name in block letters); that by six he'd already had two holes in one. No, the father knew his son would need a mind as one-piece as his swing."—*Rick Reilly, March 27, 1995*

18-Across

No. 2 Can Play

ACROSS

1 Top pitcher
4 *True ___* (movie starring "The Duke")
8 RBI producers
11 *___ the Drum Slowly*
13 18-Across was named ___ school player of the year in 1992
14 Back, on a yacht
15 One on steroids, e.g.
16 Places to perform axels and camels
18 [See photo]
20 Lawrence Berra, more famously
21 Dodge, as tacklers
25 In the cellar
29 "___ Mike" Tyson
30 Teammate of 18-Across
35 Netman Nastase
36 Eli Manning's alma mater: Ole ___
37 MLB or IOC ordinance
39 Noted Shaq ex-teammate
43 Players such as 18-Across
48 Retiree honored annually at many ballparks
51 "Hey, ___ living"
52 Down Under hopper, for short
53 Boxer's wrap
54 Many a spectator at Royal Troon
55 Pass alternative
56 Irish language
57 Jeff Gordon's NASCAR team (abbr.)

DOWN

1 "Nothing beats ___" (old beer slogan)
2 Hall-of-Famer Stengel
3 January, to Sergio García
4 Stadium rows 7-10, perhaps
5 Receiving great Jerry
6 "Oh, now ___ it!"
7 Babe Ruth's number
8 Solo in *Star Wars*
9 Washington's ___ Stadium
10 Starters at some Jesuit schs.?
12 Golfer Norman
17 Michael "The Playmaker" ___
19 Weightlifting unit, for short
22 SEC sch.
23 Anonymous John
24 WSW's opposite
26 Asset for 18-Across, in the field
27 Perform a la Ligety
28 Cobb and Law
30 Pen point
31 Melvin of the NBA
32 MLB's Nieves or Cordero
33 It makes stadium pretzels rise
34 Poses questions
38 Color of some Sox
40 Centerfielder Amos
41 Screw up
42 ___ Derby (British horse race)
44 Vizquel who's won multiple Gold Gloves
45 Parts of an iron-pumping set
46 Golf course "shot blocker"
47 H.S. exams
48 Former Knick Louis ___
49 "Sweet ___" Piniella
50 Mattingly who was the last official team captain before 18-Across

• **Answer on page 136** • • • • • • • • • • • • • • • • • •

The Rundown

BIRTHDAY June 26, 1974

BIRTHPLACE Pequannock, N.J.

FUN FACT In 1992, by the end of his senior year at Kalamazoo (Mich.) Central High, he had been contacted by scouts from 27 of 28 major league teams. The only team that hadn't reached out to him? The Yankees.

HE SAID IT In 1999, during his fifth season in the majors, of his adopted home: "This is the greatest city in the world. You always hear players say, 'I'd never play in New York.' I don't understand why you'd say that—unless you're afraid to fail."

HE ALSO SAID THIS In 1999: "My upbringing was like *The Cosby Show*. We had fun, always did a lot of things together. My parents were involved in everything my sister and I did."

STATS ENTERTAINMENT Over the last 10 years (1999–2008) he led the majors in hits (1,947) and was second in runs scored (1,115). In 2008, in Yankee Stadium's last season, he broke Lou Gehrig's record for hits in the ballpark (1,274).

FROM THE SI VAULT "He is a one-man melting pot, fittingly taking a lead role in New York. As he left Yankee Stadium after a game recently, he stopped on his way to the parking lot and signed autographs for a crowd of kids. [He] is prepared for the onslaught of autograph gnats and collectibles pests who swarm to highly touted rookies, but he is determined not to let them ruin his days. He recently took an apartment in Manhattan, a rare move for any New York athlete, let alone someone so young. He plans to live alone, even though it makes his mother nervous. In his first season in the city he intends to see more than just his living room and his locker." —*Gerry Callahan, May 6, 1996*

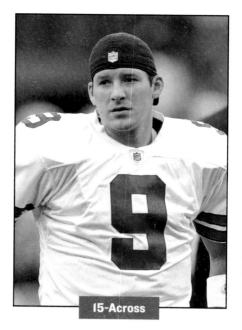

15-Across

Pass 'Em Cowboy

ACROSS

1 Judo surface
4 Stammering sounds
7 Big leagues
11 Unguarded downfield
13 Feature of Strahan's smile
14 Mardi Gras follower
15 [See photo]
17 One and a half-turn jump
18 Competing in a Volvo Ocean Race, e.g.
19 Mast-supporting cable
21 Some QB protectors
23 Game with balls and a jack
27 Words before bat and large
30 Status for 15-Across when he first signed with the Cowboys
33 Actor ___ Cobb of *The Racers*
35 "Yes, captain"
36 TCU's horned mascot
37 Player not under contract
40 Orlando-to-Miami dir.
41 Threw ___ (chucked it downfield)

42 HR king Sadaharu and kin
44 Salt-throwing sport
47 '80s Celtics star Danny
51 ___-*Tough* (football movie)
54 Eastern ___ (15-Across's college)
56 Lindros of the NHL
57 Eligibility criteria in some events
58 7-Eleven's "big" drink
59 "Look, I did it!"
60 Lumberjack's single buck tool
61 No, in Congress

DOWN

1 Outfielder/coach Manny
2 Won ___ (raked in the chips)
3 Hamiltons
4 Nickname for Evonne Goolagong?
5 Los Angeles athletes, once
6 Position the ball, after a tackle
7 Postseason game
8 2001 Heisman runner-up Grossman
9 Rugby league's drop goal score
10 5-Down's home as of 1995 (abbr.)
12 Many a Rangers fan, briefly

16 Kasey Kahne's "saucy" ex-sponsor
20 Dr. J's first league
22 Pull in, as an interception
24 NBA big guys (abbr.)
25 Co. bigwigs
26 ___ rusher (Dwight Freeney, e.g.)
27 ___ Romeo (sports car)
28 Maryland athlete, for short
29 ___ game (spectate)
31 Chicago's Jermaine
32 The Nevada Wolf Pack's home
34 Simpson linked to 15-Across
38 First Fiesta Bowl winner (abbr.)
39 Muay ___ (martial arts boxing)
43 Perform a national anthem
45 Soccer's Hamm and others
46 Korbut who did the Korbut Flip
48 Team's city or name, e.g.
49 River between 38-Down and Tucson
50 Cable TV athletic award
51 Game-match link
52 Bullpen stat
53 Shipmen prefix for Navy athletes
55 Kareem's name at birth

Answer on page 136

15-Across

Point Man

ACROSS

1 Bending locale when doing pikes
5 Slugger Sammy
9 Elevens, in craps
12 Kid's fun run distance, briefly
13 Daytona ___ Speedway (abbr.)
14 Auburn Univ. rival
15 [See photo]
17 "Nothing but ___!"
18 "___ showers!"
19 Se Ri ___ (1998 U.S. Women's Open champ)
21 Shaq's is a size 21
22 Team that drafted 15-Across fourth overall in 2005
26 15-Across's college
28 Popular savings plan
31 Big initials in bowling equipment
32 Linebacker's role, sometimes
33 22-Across's home
38 Rack complement in 8-ball
39 Bartender's question: "What'll ___?"
42 ___ Enterprise

43 How pickles are usually packaged
45 Chum
47 15-Across was named ___ of the Year for the '05-06 season
50 Baseball's Hodges
51 Woody's folk-singing son
52 "___ mouse!"
53 Alcott of the LPGA
54 There's no gain without it, supposedly
55 Barcelona women (abbr.)

DOWN

1 Golfer Scott
2 "A legend ___ own time"
3 Royal ___ Yacht Club (1987 America's Cup defender)
4 Rope on a bunny slope, e.g.
5 1980 NFL MVP Brian
6 Is ___ roll
7 Barnes of the NHL
8 The AP NFL ___ Team
9 Baseball team known as the Highlanders from 1903 to 1912

10 The ___ Miss Rebels
11 Didn't play
16 Former Mets home
20 "Gimme ___!" (Rutgers cheer start)
22 Tough guys
23 Rolled ___ pick
24 Dosage amt., perhaps
25 Pigpen
27 Curly-leafed vegetable
28 Brahms's *Symphony No. 3 ___ major*
29 Outdoors/sporting goods company
30 How a total loser performs
34 Extra five-min. periods for 15-Across
35 Fasten a chin strap, again
36 Espinosa who became a Met at age 17
37 Philly's Hawks
40 Reds manager Dusty
41 Eleniak of *Baywatch*
43 Start of a famous triathlon?
44 The Mediterranean and Baltic
45 Org. with many below-par events?
46 Position an air rifle
48 Many saw Brandy Chastain's
49 Will Smith role

17-Across

"Boom!" Guy

ACROSS

1 Game of grips, chips and yips
5 ___ Poly (university for 17-Across)
8 Customized vehicle for 17-Across
11 Olympic runner Zátopek
12 Stadium buy that's often half ice
13 Suffix with ranch
14 Hockey's Phil, familiarly
15 "America's Sexiest Sportscaster" Andrews, according to *Playboy*
16 Give it ___ (try)
17 [See photo]
20 Split off from the band
23 Legal suffix
24 Mendes of *2 Fast 2 Furious*
25 Junkyard dog's warning
27 Big Apple site for NHL and NBA games
30 Player for Coach 17-Across
35 "Nice guys finish last" Durocher
36 Green stuff near the Green Monster
37 ___ *Given Sunday*
38 John, at Manchester United games
41 CC Sabathia, in 2009
43 Bust site for 17-Across
47 Bullfight cheer
48 ___ Mary (game ender, sometimes)
49 2006 home of *Monday Night Football*
53 First network for 17-Across
54 Goose ___ (undesirable scores)
55 Like Olympic marathoners
56 Owns
57 NFL sack artists
58 College with a bulldog mascot

DOWN

1 "___ whiz!"
2 Meditation syllables
3 35-Across nickname: "The ___"
4 Olympian Griffith-Joyner, familiarly
5 Husked item at Nebraska
6 Stop on ___
7 Actresses Turner and Wood
8 It hooks inside a bicycle rim
9 Chant "C'mon!," e.g.
10 Shortly
12 Former Giants player Jason
18 1972 Olympic darling Korbut
19 Moore of *A Few Good Men*
20 Former Metro automaker
21 NASCAR circuit
22 Hot shot in Nagano?
26 Fight segments (abbr.)
28 Home state of the Summit League's Jackrabbits (abbr.)
29 The G of "GU" on '08 NFL uniforms
31 Lounge
32 A "Pine Tar Incident" team
33 Morrison who was a No. 3 NBA pick
34 Some whiskey
39 Reacted to a big air stunt, perhaps
40 Old enough to vote
42 Bruins great Cam
43 1989 Masters runner-up Scott ___
44 Jessica of *The Love Guru*
45 "Great Taste... ___ Filling" (ad line of old for 17-Across)
46 Newton fillers
50 Body for body surfers
51 Chum
52 SSW's opposite

· **Answer on page 136** ·

The Rundown

BIRTHDAY April 10, 1936

BIRTHPLACE Austin, Minn.

FUN FACT He traveled by train for the first eight years of his broadcast career, but switched to the bus in 1987, in part because he couldn't always easily get to Amtrak stations. The first Madden Cruiser, supplied by Greyhound, cost $480,000 and was outfitted with a bed, a shower, two telephones, an intercom system, two VCRs and a pantry. In return for it, Madden made stops around the country to meet Greyhound employees.

HE SAID IT In 2002, about the bus: "Mike Tyson is the only person who ever asked me how fast the thing can go. I told him, I don't know, you know, we're not drag-racing 18-wheelers across Montana."

HE ALSO SAID THIS In 1985, on why he quit smoking and switched to chewing cigars: "They taste great, and they're less filling."

STATS ENTERTAINMENT In 10 season as an NFL coach his record was 103–32; his .763 winning percentage is best among coaches with 100 career wins.

FROM THE SI VAULT "He is a born communicator. His talent for putting thoughts into words that engage the attention of a particular audience and his special knack for infusing these words with his own personality have been the keys to his success not only as a broadcaster but also as a coach. Moreover, [he] listens to others as attentively as they to him. Two-way talk— good old-fashioned conversation—is his hobby. Conversation, as [he] sees it, is living and learning at the same time, and, thus, a doubly efficient way to spend one's hours. That's important to [him], because although he never seems to hurry, he rarely wastes time." —Sarah Pileggi, Sept. 1, 1983

18-Across

Spin Doctor

ACROSS

1 Five-setter, e.g.
5 Underclassmen H.S. teams
8 100m or 10K
12 Play over
13 Namath's Super Bowl
14 Score ___ (get home)
15 Surfing danger
16 Baseball base
17 Hardly a jock
18 [See photo]
21 Press passes, e.g.
22 Ohio cheerleaders ask for it twice
23 Highlands game sphere
26 Type of gold medal for 18-Across in 2008
30 Youth sports org. supported by men in blue
31 Chris Evert, a k a ___ Greg Norman
32 Post-O.R. post
33 18-Across rival
36 The Elite Eight, e.g.
38 Barista's tip collector

39 Homer Simpson exclamation
40 Grand Slam titles won by 18-Across every year from 2005 to 2008
45 "All-star" car competition, briefly
46 Detroit-based labor org.
47 Match delayer for 18-Across
49 Boxing champ's prize
50 ___ Tin Tin
51 Good place to find a pickup game
52 Entry charges
53 Common stats divs.
54 "___ we forget..."

DOWN

1 Foul up
2 Teammate, for example
3 Creative spark
4 ___ corner punt
5 Downwind sailing maneuvers
6 Urine sample collector
7 Motions, for a fair catch
8 Drug-test adjective
9 The "A" in BALCO
10 Forearm-strengthening lift

11 Tight or defensive follower
19 Gator suffix
20 "___ questions?"
23 Sunblock letters
24 ___-Bo (cardio-boxing program)
25 The ___ Course at St. Andrews
26 Eight-time Norris Trophy winner
27 Popular spot during a yellow
28 Surface for Nicole Bobek
29 Coach's final list
31 Dolphins great Morris
34 Gives a red card to
35 Did the last event in a heptathlon
36 Alley ___
37 SI swimsuit model Tiegs
39 Churchill ___
40 ___ safety
41 Jerry Maguire, for Tom Cruise
42 Abundance for Polamalu
43 Select, to an all-star team
44 Sets a setter on, say
45 WBA's cousin
48 Washington player, for short

The Rundown

BIRTHDAY June 3, 1986

BIRTHPLACE Manacor, Majorca, Spain

FUN FACTS He is naturally righthanded, but when he was 10 years old he began playing lefthanded at the urging of his uncle Toni, a former club pro who believed the switch would give him an advantage over righthanded opponents. In 2008 he became the first lefthander to finish the year ranked No. 1 since John McEnroe in 1984.

HE SAID IT In August 2005, after a loss to 19-year-old Czech Tomas Berdych which snapped his 16-match winning streak: "I don't have good luck in the match points."

STATS ENTERTAINMENT In 2005, he won 11 ATP Tour titles, breaking Mats Wilander's record of nine, set in 1983, for most victories by a teenager. His Open Era record 81-match clay court winning streak, which ran from April 2005 to May 2007, surpassed Guillermo Vilas's mark of 53, set in 1977.

FROM THE SI VAULT "[His] greatest gift might be his poise. His first breakthrough came two years ago at age 16 when he played Carlos Moya, a former world No. 1, who also hails from Majorca and served as [his] older pledge brother when the teenager rushed the ATP fraternity. Unflustered, [he] won in straight sets. ('He will become the youngest Number 1 ever,' Moya said after the match.) Today, though still scarcely older than most of the ball boys who fetch him towels, [he] may be the sport's most mentally sound player. Pumping his fists and screaming '¡Vamos!' (Let's go!), he has the enviable ability to summon his best tennis when it matters most. 'That kid,' says John McEnroe, 'is just fearless.'"
— *L. Jon Wertheim, May 23, 2005*

33-Across

Hot Wheels

ACROSS

1 Archie Manning, to Peyton
4 Tennis's Shriver
7 Sportscaster Musburger
12 Harlem Globetrotters creator Saperstein
13 Coach Parseghian
14 Round-trip taker, 755 times
15 Makes a draft pick
17 Minimal
18 Movie that famously interrupted a 1968 Raiders comeback
19 Chop block target
21 Airport inits. for the 49ers
23 Robertson and De La Hoya
27 Give a marker to
30 Olympic gold medalist Hadi Saei's country
32 Site of the '98 and '08 Olympics
33 [See photo]
36 Norse god
37 Verne's *Nautilus* captain
38 Robert Redford in ___ *Natural*
39 Blitz
41 Pair in Tennessee?
43 Auction offering
45 Merman of *Gypsy*
49 Skater Hughes who won Olympic gold
52 Web company 33-Across endorses
54 Segment of a movie
55 Pitcher Doug
56 Dusk-___-dawn
57 "___ Ray" Leonard
58 NASCAR additive
59 Victory sign

DOWN

1 Event in which Bolt bolts
2 Ali: "... sting like ___"
3 Place to order a reuben
4 Big water hazard at Pebble Beach
5 Steelers founder Rooney
6 Goalie Glenn Hall played 502 consecutive games without one
7 They're often rounded on a diamond
8 Vehicle for 33-Across
9 Pitching stat
10 "Smoking or ___?"
11 Network for Charles Barkley
16 The Ravens' Reed and others
20 The '72 Dolphins' ___ Defense
22 Syracuse U, to fans
24 "Play the ball ___ lies"
25 Coach Kotite
26 Sumo wrestler's hot drink
27 Locker room emanation, often
28 Boggs of baseball
29 *National Velvet* author Bagnold
31 King Kong, for one
34 The Brickyard's state
35 Became fit and firm
40 "None of the above" choice
42 R.R. bldg.
44 Dugout leaders (abbr.)
46 Set at many a Super Bowl party
47 Falco of *The Sopranos*
48 ___ Alzado
49 Flattening sound for Greg LeMond
50 Pressure prefix
51 "Mr. October," to friends
53 Morsel for Secretariat

• • • • • • • • • • • • • • • • **Answer on page 136** • • • • • • • • • • • • • • • •

The Rundown

BIRTHDAY March 25, 1982

BIRTHPLACE Beloit, Wis.

FUN FACTS A go-karting national champion at age 12, she was also a cheerleader in high school but was kicked off the squad. The reason? She missed too many practices because she traveled to Europe to watch go-karting championships. When she was 16 she left school to compete in the Formula Vauxhall Series in England but still earned her GED at age 18.

SHE SAID IT In 2002: "You use what you have. I'm a girl, I can promote products, and I'll use that to my advantage. But in the end it all boils down to speed."

SHE ALSO SAID THIS In 2005, when asked to name the best female driver no one has heard of: "I don't know. I never heard of her."

STATS ENTERTAINMENT On April 20, 2008, she finished 5.86 seconds ahead of Helio Castroneves in the Indy Japan 300, thus becoming the first woman to win a major open-wheel racing event.

FROM THE SI VAULT "A ball of fire since she was a toddler, [she] displayed a similar gung-ho style on the racetrack. When she was 13, during an event on the go-kart track at Lowe's Motor Speedway in Charlotte, she was in second place behind Sam Hornish Jr.—who would go on to win three IndyCar titles and the '06 Indy 500— as the two charged into the final turn. Hornish lifted off the gas; [she] didn't. She drove straight over Hornish's rear bumper, up his back, and was launched into the air. They both crashed, but a message was sent that to this day Hornish still remembers: [She] does not back down."
—*Lars Anderson, May 19, 2008*

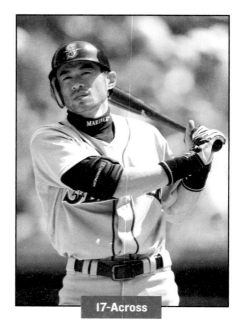

17-Across

Slew of Hits

ACROSS

1 Like LPGA players (abbr.)
4 Do or say ending of old
7 NBA All-Star Game network
10 Kovalchuk of the NHL
12 Prefix with classical
13 ___-in (tournament lock)
14 Gang Green
15 Average golfer's 180-yard club
17 First name on the back
of a Mariners jersey
19 17-Across's last name
20 ___ Love of the Game
21 L.A. to Denver dir.
22 Leisurely run
25 Bullpen standout
27 Randy "Big ___" Johnson
31 Type of homer 17/19-Across hit in
the 2007 All-Star Game (a first)
35 Gym apparatus
36 NHL trophy, e.g.
37 Prefix with thermal
38 Like 17/19-Across's uniform number

41 Clinch breaker
43 Robinson who, like 17/19-Across, led in
steals and batting avg. for a season
46 American ___ (17/19-Across milieu)
50 Giambi or Abreu
52 Stadio Olimpico site
53 Do in, as a dragon
54 A batting helmet protects it
55 League standouts
56 "___-Hut!"
57 MLB twin killings, briefly
58 Former JFK lander

DOWN

1 Vijay Singh's homeland
2 JumboTron "juice" (abbr.)
3 Muscle can turn to fat, e.g.
4 Implement, as a rule
5 Race car driver Fabi
6 Take it to the ___
7 Drive-___ window
8 Breakfast area
9 Basketball's Kukoč
11 "Like that's gonna happen"

13 Assess, as an opponent
16 Go, on a pitch
18 "___ to the Final Four"
22 Triangular sail
23 Impossible final NFL point total
24 Fed. property overseer
26 List-ending abbr.
28 Racehorse, slangily
29 Anger
30 Ring decision
32 Reassurance after a fall
33 Pitchers
34 Sport where touches are scored
39 Noise
40 Faked, in hockey
42 ___ club (AAA team, perhaps)
43 Make jokes
44 Formula One shaft
45 Printer's blue color
47 State execs
48 Ball counters
49 ___ Lansing, home of the Spartans
51 Initials of the poet after whom
a Ravens mascot is named

11-Across

Flair in the Air

ACROSS

1 Cleared the puck, illegally
5 Winter ___ Tour
  (series for 11/56-Across)
8 ___ Bull (11/56-Across sponsor)
11 [See photo], with 56-Across
13 Level below the majors
14 Lumberjack's block chop implement
15 ___-Croatian
16 They line up outside TEs
17 QB McMahon
18 Nickname for 11/56-Across
21 The Wizards' home (abbr.)
22 Cry's companion
23 Old-time actress West
25 East or West suffix
27 Lions and Tigers and Bears
31 Airer of some Olympic events
33 Titans' org.
35 'Vette roof option
36 Buffalo wing?
38 Cornerback Ty
40 ___ & Perrins

41 Shrink
43 Philbin's co-host
45 Sport for 11/56-Across
50 Foul ___
51 Goad, with "on"
52 Outfielder Vélez and S.U's mascot
54 One who's thrown, in martial arts
55 Kickoff holder
56 See 11-Across
57 Hogan or Crenshaw
58 2000 Olympics mascot whose name
   is part of the host city's name
59 Colin Montgomerie, e.g.

DOWN

1 Mag. output
2 Cook-off competitor
3 Record holder for the most doubles
  in a season (he set it in 1931)
4 43rd prez's nickname
5 Cleveland's "___ Pound"
6 Sphere atop the FIFA World Cup Trophy
7 Got beat by the tag
8 The Bobcats' Bell

9 Illuminated stadium sign
10 Floor model
12 Fans often fill a stadium with it
19 Drag racing org.
20 Swimming event
23 Banquet hosts, briefly
24 Ivanovic who won 47-Down in 2008
26 CBS's *The ___ Today*
28 Part of ACC
29 Bartender on *The Simpsons*
30 Doral Golf Resort & ___
32 Rowing team
34 Austin or M.L. of the NBA
37 ___ Field (Brooklyn Dodgers home)
39 Football fan's wife on game day
42 One over
44 Cores
45 Game attendee's souvenir
46 Sponsor for Tiger
47 The French ___
48 Approached Champions Tour eligibility
49 ___ receiver (crunch time target)
53 Volleyball spike assist

Answer on page 136

I-Across

PA. Pa

ACROSS

1 [See photo], with 26-Across
4 Stare
8 50-plus org.
12 Three-point line
13 He played doubles with Ion
14 Speak unclearly
15 "___ out!" (ump's cry)
16 I/26-Across's school
18 Good thing to break in baseball
20 Yacht's rear
21 Barber or Grange
23 Jazz coach Jerry, et al.
26 See I-Across
30 Posted ___ time (was far behind)
31 Bear Bryant's team, on scoreboards
32 Swing-and-a-miss crowd reactions
34 ___ routine (perform in gymnastics)
35 Like sweaty palms
38 The I6-Across ___ Lions
41 "The ___ of Swat"

43 Super Bowl ___ was the first one played indoors
44 Football's Sayers and others
46 In-field flies?
50 Longtime position for I/26-Across
53 Got in a scull
54 ___-inflammatory
55 Vasily Alekseyev's "no"
56 Place with whirlpool baths
57 Brainchild
58 Bando and Butera
59 Big ___ (conference for I/26-Across)

DOWN

1 Toronto squad, familiarly
2 Pitcher Hershiser
3 Khaki's kin
4 Nickname in a Rockne speech
5 Newcastle Brown ___
6 I/26-Across had 359 at the end of the 2008 season
7 Hrbek and Desormeaux
8 Minute Maid Park ballplayers
9 Plimpton portrayer in *Paper Lion*

10 Chariot's track
11 ___-game show
17 Actress Ward of *The Fugitive*
19 G.I.'s Desert Storm grub
22 Crime lab material
24 Midday
25 Move in the breeze
26 Sideline reporter Oliver and others
27 Matty or Moisés
28 Party in a parking lot
29 *A League of Their ___*
33 A touchdown
36 Old arenas
37 Pool player's powder
39 Figure skater's leg coverings
40 ___ *Cup* (Costner movie)
42 Really bright colors
45 ___ few words (give some advice)
47 Mgr.'s helper
48 "Let's go to the video ___"
49 Smith or Mikita
50 ___ Karate (old aftershave)
51 Receiver
52 Original frame from *Fantasia*

· · · · · · · · · · · · · · · **Answer on page 136** · · · · · · · · · · · · · · · ·

The Rundown

BIRTHDAY Dec. 21, 1926

BIRTHPLACE Brooklyn

FUN FACT As a senior at Brooklyn Prep, his team had only one loss—to St. Cecilia in Englewood, N.J., which was coached by future NFL Hall of Famer Vince Lombardi

HE SAID IT In 1966, of a prospective recruit: "It isn't that I like the boy because he's Italian. I like him because I'm Italian."

HE ALSO SAID THIS Answering a question about whether his players would be affected by all the attention the team was receiving in advance on the 1969 season, he said, "I told them publicity is like poison—it won't hurt you if you don't swallow it."

STATS ENTERTAINMENT His 14 interceptions as a college player still earn him a share of that school's record. In 43 seasons as a head coach, he has led his team to five undefeated seasons. And since he began at his school as an assistant, the U.S. has had 12 presidents.

FROM THE SI VAULT "As this year's Sportsman of the Year, we choose a tenured professor who wears glasses thicker than storm windows, a jacket and tie, white socks and pants legs that indicate continual fear of flash floods. He goes about 5′ 10″, 165 and looks less like a football coach than a CPA for an olive oil firm. On most mornings he leaves a red Ford Tiempo in the modest driveway of the modest house he has owned since 1967 and walks to the office. He has worked at the same place for 37 years. For excitement, he likes to sit in his La-Z-Boy and doodle on a yellow sketch pad. Such a glitzy celebrity is our honoree that his number is in the book." —*Rick Reilly, Dec. 22, 1986*

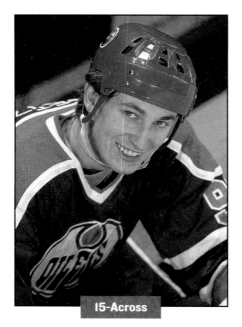

15-Across

Great Guns

¹	²	³	⁴	⁵		⁶	⁷	⁸		⁹	¹⁰	¹¹

(grid)

ACROSS

1 Little men, for Spassky
6 Pitcher Clemens, to friends
9 Marv Albert's "It's good!"
12 E's, in military communications
13 Cauliflower ___
14 ___-Star
(15/16-Across, 18 times)
15 [See photo], with 16-Across
16 See 15-Across
18 Speed skater Heiden
19 Costa ___
20 15/16-Across, from 1979 to 1988
26 Cat's cry
27 Big bird in Ian Thorpe's country
28 Longtime host of the Pebble
Beach "Clambake"
31 Loosen tangled laces
34 "That feels gooood!"
35 Fencing sword
36 Player coached by 15/16-Across
43 "Do ___ fa..."
44 Pitcher Tiant

45 Trophy 15/16-Across won 10 times
(for most points in a season)
48 15/16-Across's team, 1988 to 1996
49 Captain ___ Albano
50 15/16-Across's "office" was behind it
51 Sports awards host
52 Slash or hook suffix
53 Bonaventure and Louis preceders
54 Goes off course

DOWN

1 Bird that's a homophone
of a kid's baseball league
2 Magician's line: "Pick ___"
3 James Taylor's *That's ___ Here*
4 Sarges and some corporals
5 U-turn from NNW
6 Lengthen the rough, again
7 Put an ___ the water
(prepare to row)
8 ___-Roman wrestling
9 No. 8's Red Sox nickname
10 Antlered animal
11 Stallone, to friends

17 Doubles skater Babilonia
21 Okla. football rival
22 Westminster Dog Show group
23 Sportscaster Berman
24 Angsty rock genre
25 Zamboni erasure
28 Reds head topper
29 Cheering section syllable
30 "Well, lookie here!"
31 Shopping bars (abbr.)
32 Keanu's *The Matrix* role
33 Type of citrus pie
35 Is
37 Drop a pop-up, e.g.
38 Some bright fish
39 "O.K., go ahead and serve"
40 Approximate weight
of a squash ball
41 Comerica Park player
42 Twisty road sections
45 Boxer Laila
46 Artest or Swoboda
47 Relief pitcher McGraw
48 Boston's Garnett, familiarly

Answer on page 136

The Rundown

BIRTHDAY Jan. 26, 1961

BIRTHPLACE Brantford, Ont.

FUN FACTS He played in every All-Star game held during his career. He is the first NHL player to have his number retired league-wide; no one can ever wear No. 99 again.

HE SAID IT In 1986, when asked about fighting in the NHL: "Sometimes people ask, 'Are hockey fights for real?' I say, 'If they weren't, I'd get in more of them.'"

HE ALSO SAID THIS In 1993, on reaching the Stanley Cup finals: "You know you've come a long way when you look at the out-of-town scoreboard and there are no scores."

STATS ENTERTAINMENT He first set the single-season mark for assists in 1980–81 (109), then broke his own record eight times. He is the only NHL player to win an individual season award at least nine times—and he has done it with two different awards.

FROM THE SI VAULT "As youngsters, most athletes who become superstars are blessed not only with extraordinary coordination but also with other physical advantages, such as exceptional size, strength and speed. All they lack are experience and the insight that derives from it. [He], on the other hand, has been, as Longfellow wrote of Hiawatha, 'learned in all the lore of old men' since his early teens. His speed was average, his size and strength below average, but his coordination and aptitude for his sport were so advanced that by the time he was 19 he had proved himself to be the best hockey player in the world. Still, as he matured physically, there was more to come." — *E.M. Swift, Dec. 27, 1982*

28-Across

Court King

ACROSS

1 Coach Willingham and others
4 "IF3" on a baseball scorecard
9 Radio V.I.P.s
12 Massage response
13 The Fighting ___
 (28-Across's high school team)
14 Players' advocate, briefly
15 With 45-Across, drafter
 of 28-Across in 2003
17 Ctry. where camogie is played
18 Final Four game
19 Hard ___ rock
20 Three-fingered saluter's org.
21 The Ivy League's Quakers, for short
23 "Telephone pole" tossed by Scots
25 German cycling great Bölts
27 Actress Tomlin
28 [See photo]
32 Remote control batteries
33 Quick, in-fight bite for Tyson
34 "Steady ___ goes"
35 Archer/actress Davis

39 Sportscaster Summerall
40 Brock known for stealing
42 "Be ___ Mike" (Gatorade slogan)
44 Pub quaff
45 See 15-Across
47 Type of 35mm cam.
48 Blast, as loudspeakers
49 Pitcher and coach
 Ellis "___" Deal
50 NCAA backcourt violation count
51 Chip dip with zip
52 Robinson's 7-Down rank
 at graduation (abbr.)

DOWN

1 Tic ___ (mints)
2 The Bulldogs sch.
3 Curly's Three Stooges
 replacement
4 Pirates great Traynor
5 Magic home
6 Soccer's Sundhage
 and singer Zadora
7 David Robinson's sch.

8 Prof.'s degree
9 Bring the ball up court, e.g.
10 Unarmed NBA coverers?
11 A javelin, basically
16 Compete
22 Treat carefully, as an injury
23 County with a hurling team
24 Prepare to shoot, in a biathlon
26 28-Across was the number ___
 pick in the 2003 NBA draft
28 The Explorers of Philadelphia
29 Conference for 28-Across
30 Scrooge's cry
31 Southern University athletes
34 In ___ life (previously)
36 Peyton's brother
37 Flower girl, often
38 28-Across's Ohio birthplace
40 In ___ land (spacey)
41 Running track
43 *Guinness World Records* suffixes
45 *The NFL Today* network
46 Winning pitcher in the
 1984 All-Star Game, Charlie ___

The Rundown

BIRTHDAY Dec. 30, 1984

FUN FACTS He is the youngest player ever drafted first overall in the NBA and the youngest player to score 50 points in an NBA game. He is also the youngest player to record a triple double, which he did when he was 20 years and 20 days old.

HE SAID IT After signing a $90 million contract with Nike and before being selected with the top pick in the draft: "I don't need too much. Glamour and all that stuff don't excite me."

HE ALSO SAID THIS In 2002, as a high school junior: "I'm under a super microscope. But I've got my friends to keep me cool and I know I can rely on them. As long as you've got friends, you've got nothing to worry about."

STATS ENTERTAINMENT During the 2007–08 season, he became the first player since Magic Johnson in 1988 to have triple doubles in consecutive days twice in the same season (in November and again in February). After only six pro seasons he was already his franchise's leader in points scored, free throws made and steals.

FROM THE SI VAULT "His voice and cadence sound eerily like Jordan's: clipped, definitive, rising at the end to signal a finality of discussion. Like Jordan, [he] also peppers his speech with references to his endorsers (or knocks on the competition) that are nearly too perfect, as if written by an ad exec. Before a game he was told that Sacramento Kings forward Francisco Garcia had sprained his ankle in trying to retrieve a ball stuck next to the rim. [His] response: 'Oh, no. Oh, wow. That's not good at all.' *(Pause for comic effect, smile.)* 'It was probably those Reeboks he had on.' *(Cue media laughter.)*" —Chris Ballard, April 24, 2006

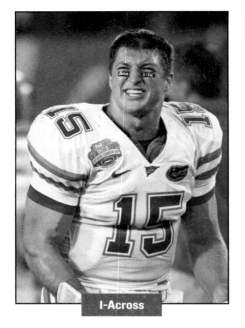

I-Across

Double Trouble

ACROSS

1 [See photo], with 19-Across
4 Deplete, as one's energy
7 Jacksonville pro, for short
10 Nutrisystem ___ (plan endorsed by Marino and Shula)
12 ___-la-la
13 Discard the top card, in poker
14 Charlie Brown's missed-kick utterance
15 "___ the fields we go..."
16 Actress Thompson or Watson
17 *Chariots of Fire* filming site
19 See I-Across
20 I/I9-Across's college team
24 Lake near Squaw Valley
25 The ___ Hey Kid
26 Mooch
28 2007 AP ___ of the Year (honor won by I/I9-Across)
33 Rudy's coach in *Rudy*
35 Beethoven's ___ *Joy*
36 Award I/I9-Across won as a sophomore

41 Boxing glove unit
42 N.Y. Cosmos' org.
43 Nabisco cookie
44 Not have one's A game
45 Coveted Indy position
49 Base for Dennis Conner
50 Emulate Franz Klammer
51 Colors
52 Ex-jet no longer visiting N.Y.
53 Like the Omaha Royals
54 20-Across's league, briefly

DOWN

1 I/I9-Across both threw and ran for over 20 of these in 2007 (abbr.)
2 *Rocky* ___ (with Mr. T)
3 Mallon of the LPGA
4 Wasn't broken, as a record
5 Madison Square Garden and the Staples Center
6 Respectable result at Bethpage Black
7 NY offensive tackle Elliott
8 Jousting garb
9 Chews like a beaver

11 Charlize of *The Legend of Bagger Vance*
13 V8 vegetable
18 Outcome that leads to overtime
19 Lawrence and Jason of the NFL
20 NBA one-pointers
21 One of 200 at the Indy 500
22 "My, my, what's this!"
23 Space between linemen
27 Open ___ (modern tennis designation)
29 Coaching legend Rupp
30 "I reckon so"
31 Golden anniversary suffix
32 Hobbs in *The Natural*
34 First woman since Babe to play in a PGA event
36 Bucket-making game
37 Yanks' Ryder Cup foes
38 Lifeless
39 Jackie "The Flying ___" Stewart
40 Shire of *Rocky*
44 Mean ___ snake
46 Courage suffix for Ted Turner
47 Golfer Trevino
48 Mac bailout key

17-Across

Red Ace

ACROSS

1 Russian doubles partner of "Swiss Miss" Martina
5 ___ check
8 Likely out in baseball
11 Bowen or Gomes of the NBA
12 "Arrivederci ___"
13 ___ station (marathon table)
14 Payment for Phil Hellmuth
15 Shortstop Vizquel
16 Barbecue sound
17 [See photo]
20 Battled ___ draw
21 Mil. jet locale
22 Jersey accompanier for the Devils?
25 Some Olympians, nowadays
28 Site of the Banzai Pipeline
31 17-Across, when he won the 41-Across MVP award
34 Midsection muscles
35 What a red flag means at Daytona
36 Araguz who holds the record for most punts in an NFL game, 16

37 MLB's Daniels or Segrist
39 The Jayhawks, on a sports ticker
41 2003 matchup between the Yankees and the 31-Acrosses
46 Lucy of *Kill Bill: Vol. I*
47 Sneaker problem
48 Org. that Myles Brand heads
50 Swimsuit Issue cover model Carol
51 Verbs for Popeye
52 *On ___ Ice: The Tai Babilonia Story*
53 Hi-speed sports cars
54 Powerade colorer
55 Half nelson, for one

DOWN

1 One of Knute's successors
2 Border Manhattanites cross on the way to Giants Stadium (abbr.)
3 Int'l. military alliance
4 Have ___ egg (save)
5 Ballpark pentagon
6 Popular PC alternative
7 Iditarod cover-up
8 Heat from 17-Across

9 Tilt, as a yacht
10 Stat units for an RB
12 Jason ___ of *Little Big League*
18 Southwestern tribe
19 Get an ___ effort
22 Vikings' grp.
23 *Evil Woman* band, briefly
24 Training sessions
26 Bit in Big Brown's bucket
27 Cooking devices for ribs
29 Speed
30 One, at the 1992 Summer Olympics
32 Dump a jockey, perhaps
33 On ___ with (equal to)
38 Former Michigan coach Carr
40 When the 49th out occurs
41 "___ the Stilt"
42 Omaha Beach event
43 "Give him ___ air"
44 Canyon comeback
45 Spinnaker, e.g.
46 Prebreak pool shot
49 *Love ___ Basketball*

I-Across

Gold Russian

ACROSS

1 [See photo], with 22-Across
6 7' 6" Ming
9 Big D basketball player
12 ___ for the Ride
13 Top left PC key
14 Pasta ending
15 ____ Center (Jazz arena, once)
16 Ultimate degree
17 Part of the Padres' and Spurs' homes
18 Lip application for Sasha Cohen and Johnny Weir
20 Texas Hold 'Em chits
22 See I-Across
26 1964 defeater of Sonny
30 Animal fat
31 ___ Bowl, played in Honolulu
32 Stat for "Smokin' Joe"
34 Author ___ Stanley Gardner
35 Placekicker Vinatieri
36 Limited ___
38 I/22-Across's first Grand Slam title
41 "Long John" of the PGA
42 Competed at Indy
46 Youth sports org.
48 National anthem contraction
50 One-run homers
52 Highway stopover
53 ___-hoo (drink Yogi once endorsed)
54 The ___ Eight
55 Center Smits
56 Letters after Hillary Clinton's name from 2001 to 2009
57 Camera endorsed by I/22-Across

DOWN

1 Alex "The ___ Duck" Karras
2 Ran ___ (took part in a relay)
3 Move like a bowling ball
4 Make it ___ the playoffs
5 Andre of tennis
6 Currency for Sadaharu Oh
7 Up and moving
8 Lorena of the LPGA
9 The Tigers of the Big 12
10 I-Across rival Ivanovic
11 Sportscaster Scully
19 With "out," a scoreless game
21 The "Miracle on Ice" at the 1980 Olympics, e.g.
23 Invited
24 Drome prefix for track cyclists
25 Got ___ from the judges
26 Cheekful for a pitcher
27 Dominant carmaker at the 24 Hours of Le Mans since 1999
28 Tomahawk, e.g.
29 National dance of Ronaldinho's country
33 ___ Eaters (sneakers insert)
37 "Be right there!"
39 "Little Poison" Waner
40 CBS Sports Spectacular, once called ___ Sports
43 Coke or Pepsi
44 Tiger's wife
45 "What can I ___ convince you?"
46 Televise, as a game
47 "Gimme ___!" (Iowa cheer)
49 Hall-of-Famer Campanella
51 N.J. title for Bill Bradley, once

Answer on page 137

The Rundown

BIRTHDAY April 19, 1987

BIRTHPLACE Nyagan, Siberia, Russia

FUN FACTS She played in her first professional tournament when she was 14—but she had signed her first marketing deal, with Nike, when she was 11.

SHE SAID IT In the spring of 2005, after being voted one of PEOPLE's 50 Most Beautiful People: "It's nice to be one of the most beautiful people. But when you step on the court, you either notice the people looking at you or you don't. I don't."

SHE ALSO SAID THIS During the summer of 2006, when, as a star of many TV commercials, she was asked if she would consider a career in acting: "I can't say I don't like acting, but I can't imagine a career when I have to spend 70 percent of my time in a trailer eating Snickers bars."

STATS ENTERTAINMENT In August 2005, she became the first Russian woman to earn the WTA's No. 1 ranking, a spot she has held for 17 weeks over the course of her career.

FROM THE SI VAULT "Perhaps there's something distasteful about this packaging and commodifying of a 17-year-old, about adults two and three times [her] age wearing her likeness on T-shirts, but it's the realpolitik of tennis. There's a reason that [she] stands to make $10 million in endorsements this year while Anastasia Myskina—also Russian, also a recent Grand Slam champion, but nowhere near as marketable—would go unrecognized walking down the main drag of your town. Not for nothing was [she] the most popular Yahoo! search term after J-Lo and Britney Spears last week. 'It's simple,' she puts it smartly. 'If you don't like the attention, don't win.'" —*L. Jon Wertheim, July 26, 2004*

18-Across

Pass Master

ACROSS

1 Boxer's training tool
4 The Crimson Tide, familiarly
8 Line up, in archery
11 Temple athletes
13 "Yikes!"
14 18-Across has thrown for a record 464 of these in the NFL
15 Billabong Pro ___ (Hawaiian island)
16 Visitor, at the 2008 Ryder Cup
18 [See photo]
20 Brees or Bledsoe
21 ___ the Eagle (British ski jumper)
25 The Gaels of New Rochelle
29 Not ___ (zip)
30 18-Across during his first NFL year
35 Bassmaster Classic equipment
36 Splinter group
37 Joakim Noah was one
39 They're pulled in crew
43 18-Across, impersonally
48 City where 18-Across made his first of 269 consecutive NFL starts

51 Kentucky's ___ Arena
52 First and ___
53 Rich who pitched for the Royals in the 1980 Series
54 "Go easy ___, fellas"
55 Roulette bet
56 Speedy Atl. crossers, once
57 The 76ers' J and others

DOWN

1 Heave from 18-Across
2 MVP, for one
3 Model assembler, at times
4 Jerky meat
5 Water for Alberto Juantoreña
6 Sportscaster Albert
7 Love to bits
8 Carbo-loaded, e.g.
9 Home state of college football's Vandals and Broncos (abbr.)
10 AOL alternative
12 Barcelona, for the 1992 Olympics, e.g.
17 Bicycle crank attachment
19 Minnesota ballplayer

22 Dwight Gooden's nickname
23 "That's something ___ longer do"
24 Dusk, in poetry
26 5th quarters in the NFL
27 St. Andrews turndown
28 K.C. Chiefs grp.
30 Manu Ginóbili's country (abbr.)
31 Brewed beverage
32 Tennis call
33 Unguarded, on the gridiron
34 Comment suffix for Jim McKay types
38 Levels in a ladder tournament
40 '70s hairdo for Julius Erving
41 18-Across went in the second ___ of the 1991 NFL draft
42 ___ Bowl XXXI (victory for 18-Across)
44 Wall St. degrees
45 The Ravens' home (abbr.)
46 Pairs locked in a staredown
47 They can reach 8,000 in drag races
48 Classic muscle car
49 St. John's ___ Storm
50 Target for 18-Across

The Rundown

BIRTHDAY Oct. 10, 1969

BIRTHPLACE Gulfport, Miss.

FUN FACT His first NFL completion went for -7 yards. And who caught the pass? He did, grabbing a batted ball out of midair.

HE SAID IT In 1993, after his first season as an NFL starter: "Reporters would ask me where I got my arm. I always thought it was from my father, but now I think I got it from my mother. She got mad at me last summer and threw a pastrami sandwich and hit me in the head. Hard. She really had something on that sandwich."

HE ALSO SAID In 2007, when asked to choose a favorite football memory: "If I were to make a list, I would include the interceptions, the sacks, the really painful losses. Those times when I've been down, when I've been kicked around, I hold on to those. In a way those are the best times I ever had, because that's when I've found out who I am. And what I want to be."

STATS ENTERTAINMENT Among the career NFL records that he holds: passing attempts, completions, passing yards, 3,000-yard seasons and touchdown passes.

FROM THE SI VAULT "The nature and number of clichés [he] attracts would make for a potent drinking game. And since he himself has long since sworn off, hoist a few in his honor. Drink a shot of redeye when you hear *gunslinger.* A dram of rum for *swashbuckler.* . . . Drink a mug of Ovaltine when you hear *He looks like a kid out there.* Chug whenever you hear *He's just trying to make something happen* or *He threw that one off his back foot.* And if you're a Packers fan, drink a double shot and turn off the television when you hear *He tried to force that one in there.*" —*Jeff MacGregor, Dec. 4, 2006*

30-Across

Pool Hustler

ACROSS

1 30-Across, in the 2000 and 2004 Olympics, e.g.
5 Toppers, such as Cosell wore
9 Saline solution drips, briefly
12 Singer Guthrie
13 From the beginning
14 The Engineers' sch.
15 "The ___ Bullet" (30-Across moniker)
17 Sugar suffix
18 UNLV's runnin' athletes, for short
19 The ___ Rally (famed auto race)
21 Suit supplier for 30-Across
24 Warm the bench
25 "Are you a man ___ mouse?"
26 Least competitive
30 [See photo]
34 Blows out
35 Up and back, for 30-Across
36 Sick
37 2004 Olympics site
40 Football ref, slangily
43 Soothing lotion ingredient
44 Judo belt
45 One of eight that 30-Across brought home from Beijing
50 Beijing Olympics broadcaster
51 Bruin nickname of note
52 ___ Placid (Olympics site)
53 Route through a chicane, perhaps
54 Takes to court
55 Unforeseen glitch

DOWN

1 Bar bill
2 Modern ___
3 Building wing
4 Dame preceder
5 Stallone role
6 Ones, to Trevino
7 Host ctry. of the 1936 Olympics
8 Like Sörenstam or Stenmark
9 "Don't worry about me"
10 Card endorsed by 30-Across
11 Drag ending for "Big Daddy"
16 What Y becomes in the past tense
20 End in ___ (draw)
21 "You've got ___ nerve!"
22 Grand ___
23 Per person
24 Fall runner, in New England
26 2002 British Open champ
27 Swimsuit model Macpherson
28 6′ 7″, for 30-Across's arms
29 Recipe amts.
31 What many swimmers remove
32 Target audience for *Madden NFL 09*
33 Long, slippery swimmer
37 Gucci and Ray
38 Kite often seen swinging
39 They make a first impression for long jumpers
40 Red or end follower, in the NFL
41 Recedes, as a tide
42 Some pens
43 ___ d'Huez (Tour de France stage)
46 The Buckeyes' sch.
47 Dierdorf of *Monday Night Football*
48 Letters preceding a nickname
49 4 x 100m segment

The Rundown

BIRTHDAY June 30, 1985

BIRTHPLACE Baltimore

FUN FACT When he won his record-setting eighth gold medal at the 2008 Olympics in Beijing, the broadcast audience included an estimated 15,000 people watching on the videoboard at M&T Bank Stadium in Baltimore; fans had stayed after a Ravens-Vikings preseason game to watch the race.

HE SAID THIS After winning that eighth medal, on what he was planning to do next: "I'm going to sit on the beach and do nothing. I'm sleeping in. I'm putting on weight. And I'm not going to care."

STATS ENTERTAINMENT At the '08 Olympics 87 countries won medals, but only eight (China, the U.S., Russia, Great Britain, Germany, Australia, South Korea and Japan) came away with more gold than he did.

FROM THE SI VAULT "[He] remains an ordinary kid suddenly leading an extraordinary life, and he works hard to maintain some balance. His agents always ensure that there is security on hand to help him navigate big public appearances, but otherwise [he] likes to travel unencumbered; that morning he had taken a train up from Baltimore by himself, only partially disguised by a droopy, Spitzian moustache that he was overly proud of (and later would be crestfallen to have to shave off to look presentable for an awards show). [He] sat undisturbed in a commuter car as he fiddled around on his laptop with a Wi-Fi card, and upon arriving in New York he made his way through Penn Station and flagged down a yellow cab on the street without a single autograph request, a 21st century Mr. Smith arriving in his Washington, with iPod." — *Alan Shipnuck, Dec. 8, 2008*

CROSS

How many goals did the U.S. score in the "Miracle on Ice" game?
Page 44

What is Reggie Miller's NBA three-pointer career record?
Page 65

S T A T S

A MATCHUP OF SPORTS AND STATISTICS

In what year did the Angels
win the World Series?
Page 40

How many Grand Slam events
did Bjorn Borg win?
Page 62

CROSS STATS by Mike Baranack

How to Solve a Cross Stat Puzzle

There are two ways to fill in the grid:

1. Answer the questions, much like a crossword (except all the answers are numbers).
2. Do the math. The digits in each row or column add up to the red numbers at the end.

For example, look at the Across clues for row B in the puzzle below. The answer to the first question, about the maximum number of games in a World Series, is fairly simple (7), so you put that digit in the first box. The next clue, about the longest return of a missed field goal, is tougher. But even if you don't remember the specifics of the play, you can still assume that the answer is between 100 and 109 yards (because you need three digits to fill out the row, and because runbacks can't be longer than 109 yards). That enables you to fill in the second and third boxes, with a 1 and a 0. The red number at the end of row B tells you that the digits in row B add up to 17, so figuring out the last number then becomes a matter of addition (7+1+0+?=17). The math tells you that the fourth box gets a 9 (and that Antonio Cromartie holds a record which will never be broken).

ACROSS

A
- NBA's longest winning streak (Lakers)
- Brooks Robinson's retired Orioles number
- Times Andre Agassi has won Wimbledon

B
- Maximum number of games for a World Series
- Longest return of a missed FG (Antonio Cromartie)

C
- Most rushing yards in a season, Division I (Barry Sanders)

D
- Most free throws made in a season (Jerry West)
- Yards penalized for illegal formation in the NFL

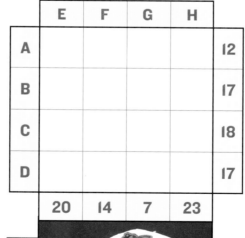

	E	F	G	H	
A					12
B					17
C					18
D					17
	20	14	7	23	

Across: A

DOWN

E
- Most FGs attempted in an NBA half (Wilt Chamberlain)
- Sports competed in at the 2008 Summer Olympics

F
- Periods in a regulation NHL game
- Most career NFL rushing TDs (Emmitt Smith)

G
- Next Super Bowl to be represented by a single Roman numeral
- Points in bowling for a spare, if it's followed by a strike

H
- Year Villanova beat Georgetown in the NCAA Final Four

	E	F	G	H	
A					11
B					21
C					23
D					8
	9	20	14	20	

Down: E

Down: F

2

ACROSS

A
- Holes in a round of golf
- Players on a cricket team

B
- Richard Petty's racing number
- Age at which Satchel Paige last pitched

C
- Year of the first Super Bowl

D
- Current number of teams in the NHL
- Uniform number shared by Michael and LeBron

DOWN

E
- Grand Slam events won by Pete Sampras
- Steve Nash's Suns uniform number

F
- Height of a soccer net, in feet
- MVP awards won by Brett Favre
- Minutes in a regulation soccer game

G
- The maroon-striped ball in pool
- NHL record for most team wins in a season (1995–96 Red Wings)

H
- Year the AL adopted the designated hitter

	E	F	G	H	
A					22
B					20
C					8
D					24
	24	27	15	8	

Across: A

Down: G

ACROSS

A
- Year Michael Jordan was drafted

B
- Players per side in a Rugby Union scrum
- Cricket World Cups to date
- Points needed to win a horseshoe game

C
- NBA titles won by the Bulls
- Laps in the Indianapolis 500

D
- Most points in a second half by an NBA team (Hawks)
- Don Drysdale's retired Dodgers number

DOWN

E
- Year of the first college football game (Rutgers vs. Princeton)

F
- Wayne Gretzky's retired Oilers number
- Points scored by Dallas in Super Bowls XII or XXX

G
- Most seasons leading the NFL in rushing (Jim Brown)
- Yard line of kickoff after an NFL safety
- Donovan McNabb's Eagles uniform number

H
- Runs scored in an MLB grand slam
- Longest NFL punt return (Robert Bailey)

4

ACROSS

A
- Seconds a rider must stay on a bull
- Events in the modern pentathlon
- Yards penalized for clipping, in the NFL

B
- Length of a bowling lane, in feet
- NFL record for longest run from scrimmage, in yards

C
- Year the U.S. hosted the men's FIFA World Cup

D
- Regulation holes in a standard PGA event
- Jim Brown's retired Cleveland number

	E	F	G	H	
A					19
B					24
C					23
D					14
	22	16	22	20	

Down: E

DOWN

E
- Super Bowl appearances by the Cowboys
- The shortstop, in official MLB scoring
- Points scored by the Giants in Super Bowl XLII

F
- The NFL's midfield line
- Record for most goals in a season (Wayne Gretzky)

G
- Year the Canadiens last won the Stanley Cup

H
- Lowest PGA score for 18 holes
- Jackie Robinson's retired number

5

ACROSS

A
- Most Formula One career wins (Michael Schumacher)
- Number of teams in the FIFA World Cup group stage

B
- Year of Tiger Woods's first British Open win

C
- Pat Tillman's retired Arizona Cardinals number
- Second most points scored in an NBA game (Kobe Bryant)

D
- Players on an Olympic volleyball team
- Consecutive times Lance won the Tour de France
- Cards in a standard poker deck

	E	F	G	H	
A					15
B					2
C					13
D					20
	21	8	16	5	

Across: C

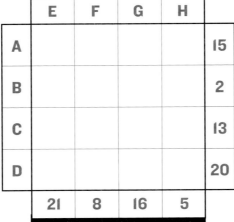

DOWN

E
- Reggie White's retired number with the Eagles and Packers
- Age at which Jack Nicklaus won his final Masters

F
- Most points scored in an NBA game (Wilt Chamberlain)
- Inning in which baseball fans stretch

G
- Number of teams in MLB
- Number of rookie winners at the Indy 500
- NHL: penalty minutes for fighting

H
- Year the Summer Olympics will be held in London

	E	F	G	H	
A					19
B					5
C					13
D					13
	16	20	10	4	

Across: B

Down: H

ACROSS

A
- Career HRs by Hank Aaron
- Number of NBA championships for the Rockets

B
- Number of lengths by which Secretariat won the 1973 Belmont
- Yards needed for an NFL first down

C
- Jimmie Johnson's racing number
- Height of an NBA rim, in feet

D
- Most consecutive MLB games played (Cal Ripken Jr.)

DOWN

E
- Most HRs in an MLB season (Barry Bonds)
- Height of men's high hurdles, in inches

F
- Number of Super Bowls won by the 49ers
- Most NFL points in a season (LaDainian Tomlinson)

G
- Most consecutive NHL games scoring (Wayne Gretzky)
- Dan Marino's retired Dolphins number

H
- Year the Angels won the World Series

7

ACROSS

A
- Unbeatable hand in blackjack
- Length of baseball's second-longest hitting streak (Pete Rose)

B
- Year Jackie Robinson made his MLB debut

C
- NBA MVPs won by Bill Russell
- Perfect game in bowling

D
- Games played in the 2008 World Series
- Mario Lemieux's retired Penguins number
- Seconds after which an NBA backcourt violation is called

	E	F	G	H	
A					11
B					21
C					8
D					25
	13	19	14	19	

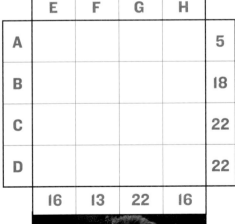
Down: E

DOWN

E
- Points for a safety in football
- Fastest tennis serve, in mph (Andy Roddick)

F
- Year of first televised sporting event (Berlin Olympics)

G
- Most Indy 500 wins (A.J. Foyt, Al Unser, Rick Mears)
- Distance between stakes in horseshoes, in feet
- Number of players per side in normal NHL play

H
- Masters wins for Arnold Palmer
- HRs hit by Mark McGwire in 1998
- Teams in Nebraska and Oklahoma's former football conference

 8

ACROSS

A
- Most inside-the-park HRs in an MLB season (Sam Crawford)
- Most steals in an NBA game (Kendall Gill, Larry Kenon)

B
- Most goalie saves in an NHL regular season game (Sam LoPresti)
- In Olympic boxing, minimum weight for a heavyweight, in kg

C
- Most career points, Division I basketball (Pete Maravich)

D
- Most blocks in an NBA season (Mark Eaton)
- Mickey Mantle's retired Yankees number

	E	F	G	H	
A					5
B					18
C					22
D					22
	16	13	22	16	

Across: C

DOWN

E
- LeBron James's age when he was drafted
- Earl Campbell's retired NFL uniform number

F
- Sections on a dartboard
- Original teams in the NHL
- World Series won by the Reds

G
- Year England won the FIFA World Cup

H
- Most consecutive NFL punts without a block (Chris Gardocki)

	E	F	G	H
A				21
B				11
C				18
D				17
	21	20	20	6

Across: D

Down: H

 9

ACROSS

A
- Most consecutive MLB games with a hit (Joe DiMaggio)
- Number of regular season NHL games

B
- Yard line the ball is spotted on after an NFL TD
- Games played in the 2008 NBA Finals
- Number of current NBA teams

C
- Innings in a regulation MLB game
- Maximum score on three darts

D
- Most career MLB strikeouts (Nolan Ryan)

DOWN

E
- Most consecutive PGA holes at par or better (Tiger Woods)
- Yellow-striped ball in pool
- Super Bowl wins by the Cowboys

F
- Ray Nitschke's retired Packers number
- Most consecutive NHL wins (1992-93 Penguins)

G
- NHL team points with record of W=36 L=35 OTL=11
- Terrell Owens's uniform number

H
- Year of Barry Bonds's last MVP award

10

ACROSS

A
- Points in rugby for a try and a conversion
- Number of MLB regular-season games

B
- Fouls a player can commit in NCAA basketball
- The black ball in billiards
- Minutes in an NFL half

C
- Most modern-era wins in an MLB season (Jack Chesbro)
- Dennis Rodman's Bulls uniform number

D
- Most NFL passing yards in a season (Dan Marino)

	E	F	G	H	
A					16
B					16
C					15
D					17
	21	10	26	7	

Across: C

DOWN

E
- Mickey Mantle's retired Yankees uniform number
- Holes played through Saturday in a standard PGA tournament
- Rounds in the 2009 Big East basketball tournament

F
- Peyton Manning's Colts uniform number
- Eli Manning's Giants uniform number

G
- Divisions in the NBA
- Strikes needed for a strikeout
- Highest uniform number allowed in the NHL

H
- Year the Winter Olympics will be held in Sochi, Russia

11

ACROSS

A
- Groups in the group stage of the FIFA World Cup
- Horses that have won the Triple Crown
- Bobby Orr's retired Bruins number

B
- Most career MLB doubles (Tris Speaker)
- Points for an NFL conversion

C
- Year George Foreman beat Joe Frazier for the title

D
- Fewest points scored in an NBA playoff game (Jazz)
- Most double plays grounded into in an MLB season (Jim Rice)

	E	F	G	H	
A					14
B					20
C					20
D					18
	21	23	13	15	

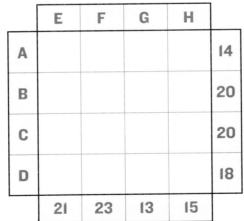

Across: C

Down: F

DOWN

E
- Reggie Wayne's Colts uniform number
- Most players that can be signed to an NBA roster

F
- Year George Foreman beat Michael Moorer for the title

G
- Most consecutive NBA seasons with more than 1,000 rebounds (Bill Russell)
- Most points scored in an NFL game (Bears)

H
- Most triples hit in an MLB game (Bill Joyce)
- Fastest race lap speed at the Indy 500 (Eddie Cheever Jr.)

	E	F	G	H	
A					12
B					23
C					22
D					8
	8	21	20	16	

Across: D

Down: H

 12

ACROSS

A
- Players on a soccer team
- Squares on a chess board

B
- U.S. Open's longest par-3 in yards (Oakmont, 8th hole)
- Number of Super Bowls in which the 49ers have played

C
- Year the Dodgers last played in Brooklyn

D
- U.S. goals in the "Miracle on Ice" game
- U.S.S.R. goals in the "Miracle on Ice" game
- Height of an Olympic diving platform, in meters

DOWN

E
- Purple-striped billiard ball
- Maximum number of clubs the PGA allows in a bag

F
- Year Montreal AAA won the first Stanley Cup

G
- Cy Young awards won by Roger Clemens
- Teams in each NBA conference that make the playoffs
- Most home runs hit by Andruw Jones in a season

H
- Most passes completed in an NFL game (Drew Bledsoe)
- Length of a FG kicked from one's own 47-yard line, in yards

13 ACROSS

A
- Points scored by Green Bay in Super Bowl I
- Muhammad Ali's total professional bouts

B
- Year of the "Black Sox" World Series scandal

C
- Most career NFL TDs (Jerry Rice)
- Points awarded an Olympic wrestler for an escape

D
- Most HRs by a player in a nine-inning MLB game
- Only number in an NBA team nickname
- Times the Heat have won the NBA championship

	E	F	G	H	
A					15
B					20
C					11
D					18
	10	21	21	12	

Across: C

DOWN

E
- TDs by LaDainian Tomlinson in 2006
- Width of a soccer goal, in feet

F
- Number of players on the floor for an NBA team
- Distance between MLB bases, in feet
- Wimbledon singles titles for Pete Sampras

G
- Most RBIs in a month (Sam Thompson)
- Years between titles when the Red Sox won in 2004

H
- Year of the first Indianapolis 500

---

14 ACROSS

A
- Most three-point attempts in an NBA game (Damon Stoudamire)
- Most NFL seasons played (George Blanda)

B
- Year of the AFL-NFL merger

C
- Rod Carew's retired number with the Angels and Twins
- Maximum number of games for the Stanley Cup finals
- Height of tennis net at middle tape, in feet

D
- Fewest team points in an NBA game (Chicago)
- Reggie Bush's Saints uniform number

	E	F	G	H	
A					11
B					17
C					21
D					20
	9	28	18	14	

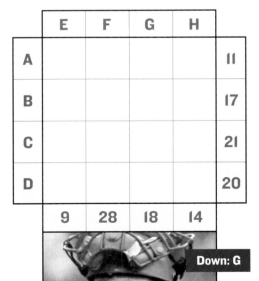

Down: G

DOWN

E
- Most offensive rebounds in an NBA game (Moses Malone)
- Jeff Gordon's racing number

F
- Year of the Spurs' first NBA championship

G
- Carlton Fisk's retired Red Sox number
- Carlton Fisk's retired White Sox number

H
- Most HRs in a season for Babe Ruth
- An eagle on a par-5
- Rings in the Olympic symbol

	E	F	G	H	
A					16
B					23
C					21
D					5
	20	20	19	6	

Across: C

Down: H

 15

ACROSS

A
- Randy Moss's Patriots uniform number
- Ray Lewis's Ravens uniform number

B
- Grand Slam events won by Andre Agassi
- Times Wayne Gretzky won the Hart Trophy (MVP)
- Minutes in a regulation NHL game

C
- Year Muhammad Ali beat George Foreman

D
- Most TDs scored in an NFL season (LaDainian Tomlinson)
- Number of pins needed for a strike in bowling

DOWN

E
- Alan Page's retired number with the Vikings
- Most Formula One wins in a season (Michael Schumacher)

F
- Year the U.S. first won the women's World Cup

G
- Lawrence Taylor's retired Giants number
- Gold medals won by Mark Spitz in the 1972 Olympics
- Points for a free throw

H
- Depth of a CFL end zone, in yards
- Super Bowl in which the Steelers beat the Seahawks

16 **ACROSS**

A
- Kevin Durant's NBA uniform number
- Points needed to win a Ping-Pong match

B
- Most MLB All-Star appearances (Hank Aaron, Willie Mays, Stan Musial)
- Times the Cowboys have been to the Super Bowl
- Rightfielder, in official baseball scoring

C
- Year the Summer Olympics were held in Munich

D
- Length of MLB's longest game, in innings
- Length of an Olympic pool, in meters

	E	F	G	H	
A					10
B					23
C					19
D					13
	8	24	21	12	

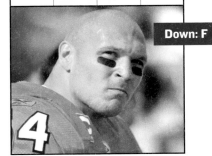

Down: F

DOWN

E
- Number of teams in the NFL
- Number of strikes needed for a 300 in bowling

F
- Brian Urlacher's Bears uniform number
- Total Olympic gold medals won by Carl Lewis
- Number of World Series won by the Dodgers

G
- Most career PGA majors won (Jack Nicklaus)
- Anniversary celebrated by the NFL in 1994

H
- Year Babe Ruth first played for the Yankees

---

17 **ACROSS**

A
- Most consecutive PGA victories (Byron Nelson)
- Colored balls at the start of a snooker game

B
- Year Texas Western beat Kentucky for the NCAA basketball title

C
- Players on a Rugby Union team
- Casey Stengel's retired Mets number

D
- The number Olympiad of the Athens 2004 Games
- Minutes in a regulation Olympic basketball game

	E	F	G	H	
A					5
B					22
C					16
D					14
	5	23	15	14	

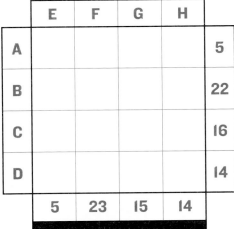

Down: G

DOWN

E
- Most NFL seasons with more than 1,000 yards rushing (Emmitt Smith)
- Distance of a soccer penalty kick, in yards

F
- Year Colts beat Giants in the "Greatest Game Ever Played"

G
- Yankees' World Series titles
- Hakeem Olajuwon's NBA uniform number

H
- Weight of a men's Olympic shot put, in pounds
- Richard Petty's wins in the Daytona 500
- Padres' World Series titles

	E	F	G	H	
A					**8**
B					**23**
C					**19**
D					**7**
	11	**18**	**6**	**22**	

Across: D

 18

ACROSS

A
- Most consecutive PGA cuts made (Tiger Woods)
- MVPs won by Emmitt Smith

B
- 2008 football documentary: *Yale Beats Harvard 29-___*
- Roy Campanella's retired Dodgers number

C
- Number of Super Bowls the Broncos have played in
- Most consecutive Wimbledon men's titles (Bjorn Borg, Roger Federer)
- Most consecutive games with an RBI (Ray Grimes)

D
- Year the White Sox beat the Astros in the World Series

DOWN

E
- Number of soccer World Cups won by England
- Most hits in an MLB season (Ichiro Suzuki)

F
- NCAA basketball: Final ____
- Roger Maris's retired Yankees number
- Anniversary celebrated by the NBA in 1996

G
- Most career MLB grand slams (Lou Gehrig)
- Yards penalized in the NFL for tripping

H
- Year Arthur Ashe won Wimbledon

Down: H

19 ACROSS

A
- Nolan Ryan's retired number with the Rangers and Astros
- UCLA men's NCAA basketball titles

B
- Most consecutive NFL games with a TD (Lenny Moore, LaDainian Tomlinson)
- Ron Guidry's retired Yankees number

C
- Year of the last MLB Triple Crown winner (Carl Yastrzemski)

D
- Minutes in a regulation NFL game
- Johnny Bench's retired Reds number
- Most consecutive MLB no-hitters thrown (Johnny Vander Meer)

	E	F	G	H	
A					9
B					22
C					23
D					13
	11	21	16	19	

Down: G

DOWN

E
- Dale Earnhardt Sr.'s car number
- Most regular-season MLB wins (2001 Mariners, 1906 Cubs)

F
- Points scored by Tampa Bay in Super Bowl XXXVII
- Bobby Hull's retired Blackhawks number
- U.S. Open wins for Bjorn Borg

G
- Most consecutive games with 100 yards rushing (Barry Sanders)
- Teams in the 2009 NCAA's men's basketball tournament

H
- NFL season in which the Dolphins went undefeated

20 ACROSS

A
- Most 3-pointers in an NBA game (Kobe Bryant, Donyell Marshall)
- Length of a snooker table, in feet

B
- Largest Super Bowl margin of victory (49ers over Broncos)
- Players in an MLB lineup
- NCAA basketball titles for Duke

C
- Most consecutive plate appearances with a walk (shared by five players)
- Most TD passes in a Super Bowl (Steve Young)
- Most assists in an NBA game (Scott Skiles)

D
- Year the Cubs last won the World Series

	E	F	G	H	
A					6
B					21
C					16
D					18
	13	22	13	13	

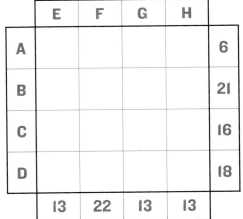
Down: F

DOWN

E
- Most INTs in an NFL season (Dick "Night Train" Lane)
- Alex Karras's Lions uniform number

F
- Barry Bonds's Giants uniform number
- Teams per conference to make the NFL playoffs
- Dan Majerle's retired Suns number

G
- Year of the first FIFA World Cup, in Uruguay

H
- Times the Avalanche has won the Stanley Cup
- Most consecutive passes without an INT (Bernie Kosar)

	E	F	G	H	
A					10
B					20
C					15
D					7
	13	16	11	12	

Across: B

Down: G

21

ACROSS

A
- Points scored by Pittsburgh in Super Bowl XL
- Kirby Puckett's retired Twins number

B
- Year Dwight Clark made "The Catch"

C
- Holes on the front side of a golf round
- Points for hitting the inner bull's-eye in darts
- Times the Ducks have won the Stanley Cup

D
- Distance of shorter Olympic hurdles race, in meters
- Innings needed for an official MLB game

DOWN

E
- Sets needed to win a woman's Grand Slam tennis match
- Most RBIs in a season (Hack Wilson)

F
- Year of Bobby Thomson's "Shot Heard 'Round the World"

G
- Singles titles at Wimbledon for John McEnroe
- Steve Largent's retired Seahawks number
- Super Bowls won by the Browns

H
- Jeff Gordon's NASCAR championships
- Most points scored in an NHL season (Wayne Gretzky)

22 ACROSS

A
- Phil Simms's retired Giants number
- Most TD receptions in an NFL season (Randy Moss)

B
- Yards penalized for offsides in the NFL
- Holes in a five-round PGA tournament
- Solid blue ball in pool

C
- Most blocks in an NBA game (Elmore Smith)
- Most team goals in an NHL game (Canadiens)

D
- Year Doug Flutie won the Heisman Trophy

	E	F	G	H	
A					7
B					16
C					15
D					22
	8	26	11	15	

Across: A

DOWN

E
- Points earned for an overtime loss in the NHL
- Most career pitching wins (Cy Young)

F
- Year the Sonics won the NBA title

G
- Barry Sanders's retired Lions number
- Players per side in Australian Rules football

H
- Babe Ruth's retired Yankees number
- Most HRs by a team in an MLB season (1997 Mariners)

23 ACROSS

A
- Medal events in the 2006 Winter Olympics
- Isiah Thomas's retired Pistons number

B
- Games in the 1997 Marlins-Indians World Series
- Dolphins' Super Bowl wins
- Fewest games to score 50 NHL goals (Wayne Gretzky)

C
- Number of players on a slow pitch softball team
- Bob Gibson's retired Cardinals number

D
- Year Texas beat USC in the BCS championship

	E	F	G	H	
A					14
B					21
C					10
D					8
	18	6	8	21	

Across: D

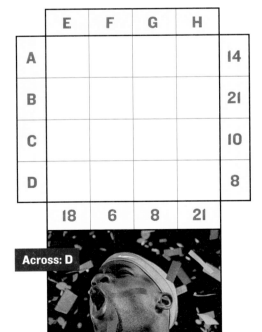

DOWN

E
- PGA record, most consecutive birdies (shared by six players)
- Red Sox's World Series titles
- Most RBIs in an MLB game (Jim Bottomley, Mark Whiten)

F
- Most punt returns for a TD in an NFL season (shared by three players)
- Most career NASCAR victories (Richard Petty)

G
- Most NFL games with 400-plus yards passing (Dan Marino)
- Tiger's front-nine score in his first Masters as a pro

H
- Year Don Larsen pitched a perfect World Series game

	E	F	G	H	
A					12
B					17
C					12
D					10
	9	23	17	2	

Across: B

Down: E

24

ACROSS

A
- Popular street basketball game, played on a halfcourt
- Par for 18 holes at Augusta

B
- Most rushing yards in an NFL game (Adrian Peterson)
- Rangers' World Series wins

C
- Total points scored in Super Bowl XXXIX (Patriots vs. Eagles)
- Yard line where the ball is spotted for an NFL kickoff

D
- Most FIFA World Cup appearances (Brazil)
- Most points in an NHL game (Darryl Sittler)

DOWN

E
- Marlins' World Series titles
- Most consecutive NFL passes completed (Donovan McNabb)
- MVPs won by Charles Barkley

F
- Year Wilt Chamberlain signed with the Globetrotters

G
- Lou Groza's retired Browns number
- Sets needed to win a men's Grand Slam tennis match
- Oscar Robertson's retired Bucks number

H
- Year the Summer Olympics were held in Sydney

25

ACROSS

A
- NHL's longest undefeated streak (1979–80 Flyers)
- In badminton, points needed to win a game

B
- Length, in yards, of dash often used to test baseball prospects
- Eric Dickerson's retired Rams number

C
- Year Tiger Woods became youngest Masters Champ

D
- Minutes in a regulation NBA game
- Dale Earnhardt Sr.'s career win total

	E	F	G	H	
A					11
B					17
C					26
D					25
	14	22	20	23	

Down: G

DOWN

E
- Most runs scored by one team in an MLB game (Cubs)
- Bob Cousy's retired Celtics number

F
- Consecutive times Arnold Palmer played in the Masters
- Mia Hamm's U.S. women's soccer number
- Lanes on an Olympic running track

G
- Most career RBIs (Hank Aaron)

H
- Year Nadia Comaneci became first Olympic gymnast to receive a 10

26

ACROSS

A
- Year USA won the Ryder Cup after trailing by four on last day

B
- Minutes in an NBA overtime period
- Most pass completions in an NFL season (Drew Brees)

C
- PGA record for most strokes under par for a round
- Points needed to win a badminton game

D
- Players on an NHL roster
- Substitutions allowed in soccer, combined for both teams
- Stanley Cups won by the Columbus Blue Jackets

	E	F	G	H	
A					28
B					13
C					7
D					11
	9	19	21	10	

Across: B

DOWN

E
- Tim Tebow's Florida uniform number
- Most College World Series titles (USC)

F
- Most career PATs made (George Blanda)
- NBA MVP awards for Larry Bird

G
- Points for a behind in Australian Rules football
- Highest MLB season batting average (Nap Lajoie)

H
- Minutes in a woman's FIFA World Cup match
- Matt Leinart's overall NFL draft position in 2006

	E	F	G	H	
A					20
B					26
C					16
D					11
	12	18	17	26	

Down: F

Down: F

27

ACROSS

A
- Chad Ochocinco's NFL uniform number
- Career shutouts for Nolan Ryan

B
- Year Magic Johnson and Larry Bird entered the NBA

C
- Most three-pointers in an NBA game (Orlando)
- Most consecutive HRs by a team in an MLB game (shared by six)
- Most TD passes in an NFL game (shared by five)

D
- Teams in the Big Ten
- Football games won by the Washington Huskies in 2008
- Ted Williams's retired Red Sox number

DOWN

E
- Dick "Night Train" Lane's Lions uniform number
- Dominique Wilkins's retired Hawks number

F
- Most consecutive shutout MLB innings (Orel Hershiser)
- Most PGA strokes under par for 72 holes (Ernie Els)

G
- Points for a hit ball clearing the boundary on a fly in cricket
- The solid maroon ball in pool
- Gale Sayers's retired number with the Bears

H
- Year the WHA folded and Wayne Gretzky joined the NHL

28 ACROSS

A
- Most 100-yard receiving games in an NFL season (Michael Irvin)
- Jack Lambert's Steelers uniform number

B
- Year of Franco Harris's "Immaculate Reception"

C
- Points for hitting the outer bull in darts
- Most consecutive Indy 500 starts (A.J. Foyt Jr.)

D
- Most rushing TDs in an NFL game (Ernie Nevers)
- Super Bowls the Packers have played in
- Yard line from which NCAA teams kick off

	E	F	G	H	
A					15
B					19
C					15
D					13
	10	19	18	15	

Down: G

DOWN

E
- Players on the field per team in the NFL
- Most NHL seasons played (Gordie Howe)

F
- Year Roger Bannister ran the first sub-four-minute mile

G
- Times Bjorn Borg won Wimbledon
- Most career MLB no-hitters
- Larry Bird's retired Celtics number

H
- Jason Witten's Cowboys uniform number
- Width of an NBA court, in feet

29 ACROSS

A
- Most consecutive NCAA men's basketball titles (UCLA)
- Most passing yards in a Super Bowl (Kurt Warner)

B
- Length of an Arena Football field, in yards
- Length of an NBA court, in feet

C
- Year of MLB's last 30-game winner (Denny McLain)

D
- Fewest team rushing yards in a Super Bowl (Patriots, against the Bears)
- Cal Ripken Jr.'s retired Orioles number
- Most seasons batting over .300 (Ty Cobb)

	E	F	G	H	
A					16
B					18
C					24
D					20
	20	21	18	19	

Across: A

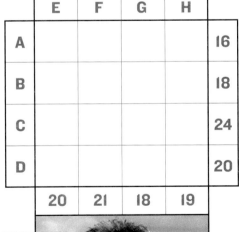

DOWN

E
- Mean Joe Greene's Steelers uniform number
- Number of men's Olympic swimming events

F
- Minutes in a regulation NCAA men's basketball game
- NFL's longest punt (Steve O'Neal)

G
- Year Wilt Chamberlain scored 100 points in a game

H
- Jerry West's retired Lakers number
- NHL teams to make the playoffs, per conference
- Points for a drop goal in Rugby Union

	E	F	G	H	
A					12
B					16
C					17
D					18
	9	26	20	8	

Across: A

Across: B

ACROSS

A
- Roberto Clemente's retired Pirates number
- Longest NFL field goal, in yards (Tom Dempsey, Jason Elam)

B
- MVPs won by Frank Thomas
- Batters in an MLB lineup
- Ernie Banks's retired Cubs number

C
- NFL record for consecutive games with a TD pass (Johnny Unitas)
- Dick Butkus's retired Bears number

D
- Year of the U.S. Summer Olympics boycott

DOWN

E
- NFL record for most TDs in a rookie season (Gale Sayers)
- Dirk Nowitzki's Dallas uniform number

F
- Year the NBA introduced the three-point shot

G
- Most HRs in a season for Roger Maris
- Record for most points by an NBA rookie (Wilt Chamberlain)

H
- Walter Payton's retired Bears number
- Most HRs in a game by one team (Toronto)

 31

ACROSS

A
- Most hits by a team in a nine-inning MLB game (1894 Phillies)
- Most turnovers by a team in an NFL game (shared by three)

B
- Number of Finals appearances for the Jazz
- Length of an NFL field in yards, including end zones

C
- Year the U.S. beat England 1–0 in a FIFA World Cup match

D
- MLB record for career HRs (Barry Bonds)
- Fewest wins in an NHL season (1974–75 Capitals)

	E	F	G	H	
A					12
B					5
C					15
D					23
	13	22	10	10	

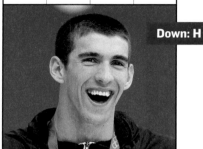

Down: H

DOWN

E
- Magic Johnson's retired Lakers number
- Most consecutive years with a PGA win (Jack Nicklaus, Arnold Palmer)

F
- Most points by an NHL player in one period (Bryan Trottier)
- Length of an extra point kick, in yards
- Football teams in the SEC West

G
- Lowest ATP ranking of a Wimbledon winner (Goran Ivanisevic)
- Bengals' Super Bowl appearances

H
- Year Michael Phelps won eight Olympic gold medals

 32

ACROSS

A
- Most consecutive NBA championships (Celtics)
- Most 400-yard passing games, career (Dan Marino)
- Stan Musial's retired Cardinals number

B
- Year of Joe DiMaggio's 56-game hitting streak

C
- Most career NHL points (Wayne Gretzky)

D
- Highest batting average for a season (Hugh Duffy)
- Most goals in an NHL game (Joe Malone)

	E	F	G	H	
A					18
B					15
C					22
D					15
	15	22	12	21	

Across: A

DOWN

E
- Most seasons leading the NFL in receptions (Don Hutson)
- Most times sacked in an NFL game (Bert Jones, Donovan McNabb, Warren Moon)
- PGA Grand Slam events

F
- Year Eric Dickerson ran for 2,105 yards

G
- Charles Barkley's retired Suns and 76ers number
- Shortest Olympic swimming event, in meters

H
- Bjorn Borg's French Open wins
- Most runs scored in a modern-day MLB season (Babe Ruth)

	E	F	G	H	
A					21
B					16
C					20
D					18
	23	22	19	11	

Across: A

Down: E

 33

ACROSS

A
- Most seasons leading the NBA in assists (John Stockton)
- NBA MVPs won by Dirk Nowitzki
- Length of Marcus Allen's record-setting TD run in Super Bowl XVIII

B
- Wins needed to make the NCAA men's basketball final
- Pitcher's usual batting order spot
- Tony Stewart's race car number in 2008

C
- Teams that make the MLB postseason each year
- Most receiving yards in a game (Flipper Anderson)

D
- Year of the first Ali-Frazier fight

DOWN

E
- Olympic gold medals won by Paavo Nurmi
- Jonathan Papelbon's Red Sox uniform number
- Chiefs' Super Bowl wins

F
- Year of Lou Gehrig's last game

G
- Most NBA regular-season victories (1995–96 Bulls)
- Total points scored in Super Bowl XXXVI (Pats over Eagles)

H
- Yard line used for the kickoff in high school football
- NHL records held or shared by Wayne Gretzky

34 ACROSS

A
- Batting position after cleanup
- Most shorthanded goals in an NHL season (Mario Lemieux)
- Formula One championships won by Michael Schumacher

B
- Year of the first Winter X Games

C
- Most yards from scrimmage in an NFL season (Marshall Faulk)

D
- Lanes used for racing in an Olympic pool
- France FIFA World Cup wins
- Width of a field hockey pitch, in yards

	E	F	G	H	
A					16
B					26
C					17
D					15
	16	15	20	23	

Down: E

DOWN

E
- British Open wins for Tom Watson
- Most MLB league batting titles (Ty Cobb)
- Largest lead in what could be called a "one-possession game" in the NFL

F
- Year last MLB player hit .400 (Ted Williams)

G
- Most free throws attempted in an NBA playoff game (Shaquille O'Neal)
- Full miles in a marathon

H
- Red Grange's retired Bears number
- Highest possible score through three frames in bowling

- -

35 ACROSS

A
- Wilt Chamberlain's NBA MVPs
- Most career MLB shutouts pitched (Walter Johnson)

B
- Diameter of an NBA hoop, in inches
- Gene Upshaw's Raiders uniform number

C
- Year Hank Aaron hit his 715th career home run

D
- NL's best season HR total between 1930 and 1998 (Hack Wilson)
- Worst starting position to win the Indy 500

	E	F	G	H	
A					6
B					18
C					21
D					20
	11	24	16	14	

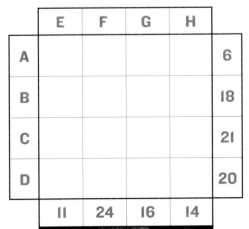

Down: E

DOWN

E
- Most triple doubles in an NBA season (Oscar Robertson)
- Bart Starr's retired Packers number

F
- Year of first modern Olympiad, in Athens

G
- Most career tennis singles titles (Martina Navratilova)
- Strokes for a birdie on a par-3

H
- Times the Buffalo Sabres have won the Stanley Cup
- Most NFL career coaching victories (Don Shula)

	E	F	G	H	
A					21
B					28
C					14
D					14
	17	25	16	19	

Down: F

Down: G

36

ACROSS

A
- Year of the first Little League World Series

B
- Carl Edwards's race car number
- Johnny Unitas's retired Colts number

C
- Most consecutive MLB seasons played (Nolan Ryan)
- Kareem Abdul-Jabbar's retired Lakers number

D
- Stanley Cups won by the Edmonton Oilers
- Minimum age to be drafted in MLB
- NBA titles won by the Denver Nuggets

DOWN

E
- Year the race car first went over 100 mph in the Indy 500

F
- Career Olympic medals won by Nadia Comaneci
- Number of the Fall Classic of Yankees vs. Mets in 2000
- Super Bowls won by the Jets

G
- Seasons Seattle had an NBA franchise before the Sonics left
- Points scored by LSU in 2008 BCS title game

H
- The number MLB All-Star Game played in 2008
- Score representing two points in tennis

37 ACROSS

A
- Most career NFL safeties (Ted Hendricks, Doug English)
- Most goals in a FIFA World Cup tournament (Just Fontaine)
- Number retired by NBA's Kings and Magic to represent their fans

B
- Secretariat's Triple Crown year

C
- Regular and postseason games won by the 2007 Patriots
- Most runners left on base in an MLB game (Yankees)

D
- Most 50 goal seasons in the NHL (Wayne Gretzky, Mike Bossy)
- Longest Super Bowl pass, in yds. (J. Delhomme to M. Muhammad)
- Angels' World Series titles

	E	F	G	H	
A					14
B					20
C					11
D					23
	15	26	17	10	

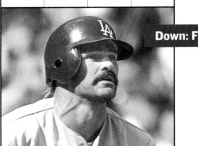
Down: F

DOWN

E
- Rounds in the NBA postseason
- Most extra-base hits in an MLB season (Babe Ruth)

F
- Year of Kirk Gibson's pinch-hit, walk-off World Series home run vs. A's

G
- Shaun Alexander's uniform number when he was with the Seahawks
- Justine Henin's age when she retired from tennis

H
- Points for a goal in Australian Rules Football
- Most steals in an NBA season (Alvin Robertson)

38 ACROSS

A
- Lou Gehrig's retired Yankees number
- Most NBA career triple doubles (Oscar Robertson)

B
- Most times walked in an MLB game (Jimmie Foxx, Walt Wilmot)
- Most assists in an NBA Finals series (Magic Johnson)
- Number of men's rowing events in the 2008 Olympics

C
- Most points in an NHL rookie season (Teemu Selanne)
- Saints Super Bowl appearances

D
- The year Johnny Vander Meer pitched consecutive no-hitters

	E	F	G	H	
A					14
B					28
C					6
D					21
	12	22	18	17	

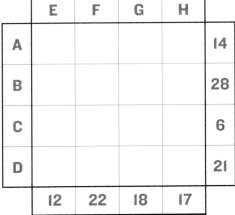
Down: E

DOWN

E
- Andy Pettitte's Yankees uniform number
- Most NBA titles for a player (Bill Russell)

F
- Year the men's NCAA Division I basketball tournament began

G
- Conference games played each season by Big Ten football teams
- Age of the NHL's oldest-ever player (Gordie Howe)
- Diameter of a baseball, in inches

H
- Most rushing yards for an NFL rookie (Eric Dickerson)

	E	F	G	H	
A					15
B					21
C					13
D					20
	14	21	21	13	

Across: A

 39

ACROSS

A
- John Elway's retired Broncos number
- Grand Slam events won by Bjorn Borg
- Most grand slams in an MLB season (Don Mattingly, Travis Hafner)

B
- Year N.C. State stunned Houston for the NCAA basketball title

C
- Number in Houston's team name before they became the Astros
- Most regular-season home wins in an NBA season (Celtics)

D
- Most consecutive NFL games lost (Tampa Bay)
- Most consecutive MLB saves (Eric Gagne)

DOWN

E
- Career HRs hit by Babe Ruth
- Number of times Uruguay has won the FIFA World Cup

F
- Year Rocky Marciano retired as undefeated champ

G
- Most receiving yards in an NFL season (Jerry Rice)

H
- Bill Russell's retired Celtics number
- Most points possible in a bowling frame
- Most double plays grounded into in an MLB game (Joe Torre, Goose Goslin)

Down: H

40

ACROSS

A
- Brian Piccolo's retired Bears number
- Most points by a player in an NBA quarter (George Gervin)

B
- Year Pete Rose was banned from baseball

C
- Most sacrifice bunts in a season (Ray Chapman)
- Reggie Jackson's retired A's number
- Most safeties in an NFL game (Fred Dryer)

D
- Countries that participated in the 2008 Olympics
- Number of minutes for a major penalty in the NHL

	E	F	G	H	
A					11
B					27
C					24
D					11
	13	17	24	19	

Across: A

DOWN

E
- Times the Tigers have won the World Series
- Most punts in an NFL game (Leo Araguz)
- Times the Knicks have won the NBA title

F
- Year Tom Dempsey kicked a 63-yard FG for the Saints

G
- Most hits by a player in an MLB inning (shared by five players)
- Most career NHL goals (Wayne Gretzky)

H
- Larry Csonka's retired Dolphins number
- Midfield yard line of an Arena Football field

Answers on page 139

41

ACROSS

A
- Minimum number of games needed to win a tennis set
- Regions in the NCAA basketball tournament
- Most team TDs in an NFL season (2007 Patriots)

B
- Number of weightlifting records set by Vasily Alexeyev
- Players on an NFL roster

C
- World Series titles won by the Phillies
- Most receiving yards in a Super Bowl (Jerry Rice)

D
- Year Nolan Ryan pitched his last no-hitter

	E	F	G	H	
A					22
B					16
C					10
D					20
	17	15	22	14	

Across: B

DOWN

E
- Height of a dartboard from the floor to center, in inches
- Most NFL games in a career with four or more TD passes (Dan Marino)

F
- Most points in an NBA season (Wilt Chamberlain)

G
- Most complete games in an MLB season (Will White)
- Joe Sakic's Avalanche uniform number

H
- Kevin Garnett's Celtics uniform number
- Super Bowl in which the Ravens clobbered the Giants
- Ozzie Smith's retired Cardinals number

	E	F	G	H	
A					22
B					14
C					19
D					20
	14	21	21	13	

Across: B

Across: D

42

ACROSS

A
- Undefeated title fight streak of Rocky Marciano
- Most career interceptions, NFL (Paul Krause)

B
- Most AL games played (Carl Yastrzemski)

C
- Total points scored in Super Bowl XXIV (49ers over Broncos)
- Consecutive seasons with 15 or more MLB wins (Greg Maddux)

D
- Year Tim Tebow won the Heisman Trophy

DOWN

E
- Maximum number of cars in a NASCAR race
- Second-longest NFL FG (Matt Bryant, Rob Bironas)

F
- Number of the Super Bowl in which the Steelers got their first ring
- NBA championships won by the Pistons
- Most consecutive MLB steals (Vince Coleman)

G
- Minutes in a Rugby Union match
- Most consecutive Stanley Cup finals (Canadiens)

H
- First year of Wimbledon

43

ACROSS

A
- Most consecutive NCAA Div. I-A football victories (Oklahoma)
- John Stockton's retired Jazz number

B
- Year the Atlanta Braves won the World Series

C
- Ronnie Lott's retired 49ers number
- Most consecutive PGA birdies
- Most Indy 500 pole positions (Rick Mears)

D
- Redskins' Super Bowl wins
- Career HRs for Willie Mays

	E	F	G	H	
A					14
B					24
C					20
D					15
	12	24	24	13	

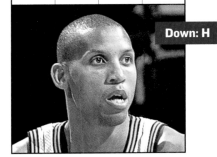

Down: H

DOWN

E
- Players on a curling team
- Most receptions in an NFL season (Marvin Harrison)

F
- Number of countries to have won the FIFA World Cup
- Most consecutive 50-or-more goal NHL seasons (Mike Bossy)
- Innings in MLB's longest game (Dodgers vs. Braves)

G
- Year Jack Nicklaus won the Masters at age 46

H
- Most career NBA three-pointers (Reggie Miller)

44

ACROSS

A
- Most rebounds in an NBA game (Wilt Chamberlain)
- Most consecutive PGA rounds in the 60s (Byron Nelson)

B
- Most interceptions thrown in an NFL season (George Blanda)
- Joe Morgan's retired Reds number

C
- Year Cassius Clay defeated Sonny Liston for heavyweight crown

D
- Points for an NBA slam dunk
- Distance to the target in Olympic archery, in meters
- Raiders' Super Bowl wins

	E	F	G	H	
A					20
B					20
C					20
D					12
	12	23	15	22	

Down: F

DOWN

E
- Most times stealing home in a career (Ty Cobb)
- Basketball teams in the ACC

F
- Pirates' World Series titles
- Years Tom Landry coached the Cowboys
- In the NFL, players required on the line of scrimmage

G
- Year of golf's first British Open

H
- Most consecutive NHL games played (Doug Jarvis)
- Strokes for an eagle, usually

	E	F	G	H	
A					10
B					28
C					17
D					16
	13	27	20	11	

Across: A

Down: H

45

ACROSS

A
- Most consecutive times reaching base in modern-day MLB (Ted Williams)
- Most offensive rebounds in an NBA game (Moses Malone)

B
- Most passes intercepted by a team in a game (Lions, Steelers)
- Length of a tennis court, in feet
- Lou Gehrig's retired Yankees number

C
- Year *Monday Night Football* debuted

D
- College football teams ranked weekly by AP
- Most triples in an MLB season (Chief Wilson)

DOWN

E
- Year Jim Thorpe won Olympic gold in the decathlon and pentathlon

F
- Most doubles in an MLB season (Earl Webb)
- Career Olympic gold medals won by Mark Spitz
- Most consecutive World Series titles (Yankees)

G
- Games won by the Mavericks in the 2006 NBA Finals
- Sidney Crosby's Penguins uniform number
- Boris Becker's Wimbledon titles

H
- Most career stolen bases (Rickey Henderson)

46

ACROSS

A
- Age of oldest Olympic medal winner (Oscar Swahn)
- Number of Notre Dame's "horsemen"
- Major championships won by Fred Couples

B
- Most games played by an NHL goalie (Patrick Roy)

C
- Minutes in an Arena Football game
- Maximum weight of a ten-pin bowling ball, in pounds

D
- Steve Smith's Panthers uniform number
- Minutes in a CFL half

	E	F	G	H	
A					14
B					12
C					13
D					20
	22	11	10	16	

Down: G

DOWN

E
- Most passing yards in a Division I football game (David Klingler)
- Most INTs thrown in an NFL game (Jim Hardy)

F
- Year Arizona Cardinals played in their first Super Bowl

G
- The number of laws of cricket
- Most consecutive NFL wins by a rookie starting QB (Ben Roethlisberger)

H
- Year the Lakers moved from Minneapolis to L.A.

47

ACROSS

A
- Most career PGA tournament wins (Sam Snead)
- Most losses to start an NBA season (1988–89 Heat, 1999–2000 Clippers)

B
- Stanley Cups won by the Bruins
- Tim Wakefield's Red Sox uniform number
- Regular-season NFL games, per team, against teams from the opposing conference

C
- Year Mike Powell broke Bob Beamon's long jump record

D
- Calendar days in the Beijing Olympics year
- NBA titles won by the Suns

	E	F	G	H	
A					18
B					22
C					20
D					15
	17	21	25	12	

Down: G

DOWN

E
- NCAA Division I-A football scholarships allowed per school
- Wilt Chamberlain's retired NBA number

F
- Most consecutive MLB games scoring a run (Billy Hamilton)
- The yellow-striped ball in pool
- Steelers' Super Bowl wins

G
- Year Michael Johnson won the Olympics 200 and 400 meters

H
- Strokes in a two-over-par round at Doral
- NFL penalty yards for offensive pass interference

	E	F	G	H	
A					18
B					16
C					16
D					14
	11	21	20	16	

Across: A

Down: G

 48

ACROSS

A
- Most rushing attempts in an NFL season (Larry Johnson)
- Most MLB seasons with 150-plus RBI (Lou Gehrig)

B
- Men's college basketball championships for North Carolina
- Michael Strahan's Giants uniform number
- Points for a goal in lacrosse

C
- Number of conferences in MLS
- Most strikeouts thrown in a modern-day MLB season (Nolan Ryan)

D
- Most FIFA World Cup appearances (Brazil)
- Minimum age on the PGA's seniors tour

DOWN

E
- NBA's longest home winning streak (Bulls)
- Most free throws made in an NBA Finals game (Dwyane Wade)

F
- Year Joe Louis beat Max Schmeling in 124 seconds

G
- Most saves in an MLB season (Francisco Rodriguez)
- Carl Yastrzemski's retired Red Sox number
- Penalty for having 12 men in the huddle, in yards

H
- Innings in a regulation high school baseball game
- Most stolen bases in a modern-day MLB season (Rickey Henderson)

49

ACROSS

A
- Number of NBA regular season games
- Goals scored in a hat trick
- NBA MVPs won by Kareem Abdul-Jabbar

B
- Jerry Rice's retired 49ers number
- Most consecutive FTs made, NBA (Micheal Williams)

C
- Most MLB HRs in a month (Sammy Sosa)
- Tom Seaver's retired Mets number

D
- Most rushing yards in an NFL season (Eric Dickerson)

	E	F	G	H	
A					19
B					24
C					7
D					8
	20	3	16	19	

Down: H

DOWN

E
- Dale Earnhardt Jr.'s current racing number
- Length of a cricket pitch in yards

F
- Year the Diamondbacks last won the World Series

G
- The number Super Bowl when the Pats beat the Eagles
- Most points scored in an NFL game (Ernie Nevers)

H
- Second-to-last round of today's NFL draft
- Winston Cup championships won by Dale Earnhardt Sr.
- Most FIFA World Cup goals scored (Ronaldo)

50

ACROSS

A
- Most seasons leading the NFL in scoring (Don Hutson, Gino Cappelletti)
- Width of the NBA lane, in feet
- Points for a takedown in Olympic wrestling

B
- LPGA's lowest round (Annika Sorenstam)
- Most points in an NBA game by a 40-year-old (Michael Jordan)

C
- Year of "The Play" in the Cal-Stanford game

D
- NFL teams in 1976
- NFL teams whose first season was 1976
- Phil Esposito's Bruins number

	E	F	G	H	
A					14
B					21
C					20
D					19
	13	27	20	14	

Across: B
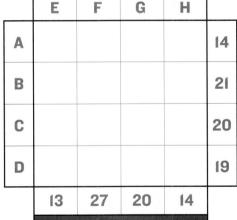

DOWN

E
- Patrick Roy's career NHL wins
- Times U.S. has won the women's FIFA World Cup

F
- Year Mark McGwire hit 70 HRs and Sammy Sosa hit 66

G
- Super Bowl appearances by the Broncos
- Length of Adam Vinatieri's winning FG in Super Bowl XXXVI, in yards
- Points an NHL team gets for an overtime win

H
- Most times walked in a season (Barry Bonds)
- Maximum games in a first-round NBA playoff series

	E	F	G	H	
A					15
B					19
C					14
D					18
	11	21	15	19	

Down: E

Down: G

 51

ACROSS

A
- Most consecutive FIFA World Cup wins (Brazil)
- Most team INTs in a season (1961 Chargers)

B
- Most team points scored in an NBA overtime game (Pistons)
- Number of tennis Grand Slam events

C
- Most career NFL completions (Brett Favre)

D
- Ernie Davis's retired Browns number
- Width of a doubles tennis court, in feet

DOWN

E
- Olympic medals won by Matt Biondi
- Strokes if you birdied every hole at Pebble Beach

F
- Year of the first Kentucky Derby

G
- Super Bowls won by coach Chuck Noll
- Divisions in MLB
- LeBron James's Cavs uniform number

H
- Most errors by a player in an MLB game (Andy Leonard)
- Most rushing yards in a Division I-A football game (LaDainian Tomlinson)

52

ACROSS

A
- Most team points scored in an NFL season (2007 Patriots)
- Dallas Stars' Stanley Cup wins

B
- The shortstop, in official MLB scoring
- Technicals needed to be kicked out of an NBA game
- Most playoff goals in an NHL season (Jari Kurri, Reggie Leach)

C
- Year the St. Louis Cardinals last won the World Series

D
- Asking price was $3 million for a ___-second Super Bowl ad in 2009
- Bob Lilly's Cowboys uniform number

	E	F	G	H	
A					23
B					18
C					8
D					14
	16	10	17	20	

Down: E

DOWN

E
- Most strikeouts by a player in an MLB game (shared by 46 players)
- Most doubles hit by a player in an MLB doubleheader (Hank Majeski)
- Shaq's shoe size

F
- Number of players for each team in a rugby scrum
- Most career NFL sacks (Bruce Smith)

G
- Length of a Ping-Pong table, in feet
- Most points scored by a team in an NBA half (Suns)

H
- Year the Summer Olympics were held in Tokyo

53

ACROSS

A
- Most career Super Bowl TD passes (Joe Montana)
- Width of a singles tennis court, in feet

B
- Most combined runs in an MLB game (Cubs and Phillies)
- Most wins in a NASCAR season (Richard Petty, Jeff Gordon)

C
- Joe DiMaggio's retired Yankees number
- Minutes in a regulation men's lacrosse game
- Number representing the center position in basketball

D
- Year Pete Rose beat Ty Cobb's alltime hits record

	E	F	G	H	
A					11
B					17
C					16
D					23
	11	25	11	20	

Across: D

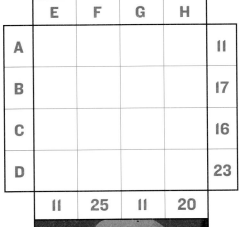

DOWN

E
- Most team grand slams in an MLB season (A's, Indians)
- Most aces in a tennis match (Joachim Johansson, Ivo Karlovic)

F
- Year Mario Andretti won the Indianapolis 500

G
- Blue Jays' World Series titles
- Longest NFL kickoff return (Ellis Hobbs)

H
- Games played in the 2001 Yankees-D'backs World Series
- Longest undefeated NHL streak (1979-80 Flyers)
- Highest par for a PGA Tour hole

	E	F	G	H	
A					15
B					25
C					17
D					8
	12	21	19	13	

Across: A

Across: B

 54

ACROSS

A
- Distance of an NBA free throw, in feet
- Yogi Berra's retired Yankees number
- Overall 2004 NBA draft position of Dwight Howard

B
- Year Joe Namath guaranteed win in Super Bowl over Colts

C
- Most MLB hits in a month (shared by three)
- Dave Winfield's retired Padres number

D
- Most FGs in an NFL season (Neil Rackers)
- Most tries in a Rugby World Cup match (Australia, 2003)

DOWN

E
- Most assists in an NBA season (John Stockton)

F
- Most goals by a defenseman in an NHL game (Ian Turnbull)
- Most hits by a player in an extra innings MLB game (Johnny Burnett)
- Most passes attempted in an NFL game (Drew Bledsoe)

G
- Steve Young's retired 49ers number
- Most points in an NBA playoff game (Michael Jordan)
- Times Florida has won the NCAA men's basketball tournament

H
- Year Fenway Park opened

55

ACROSS

A
- Most NASCAR victories in one season (Richard Petty)
- NFL penalty, in yards, for an illegal crackback

B
- Most consecutive regular season starts as an NFL QB (Brett Favre)
- NCAA basketball championships won by Georgetown

C
- Miles in the NASCAR race at the Brickyard
- Times Sandy Koufax won the Cy Young Award

D
- Year the Olympics were last held in London

	E	F	G	H	
A					15
B					18
C					7
D					22
	9	22	14	17	

Across: A

DOWN

E
- Karl Malone's NBA MVP awards
- Most Stanley Cups won by a franchise (Montreal)
- Points for an NFL PAT

F
- Pete Maravich's retired Jazz number
- Minutes in a CFL game
- Michael Jordan's Team USA uniform number

G
- Year the New York Giants refused to play in the World Series

H
- Jack Nicklaus's wins in the PGA Championship
- Pre-modern era record for stolen bases in a season (Hugh Nicol)

56

ACROSS

A
- MLB record for career hits (Pete Rose)

B
- Distance run for NFL scouting, in yards
- Matches played in a season by English Premier teams

C
- Yard line at which football's "red zone" begins
- Merlin Olsen's retired Rams number

D
- Most TD passes in an NFL season (Tom Brady)
- Tony Gwynn's retired Padres number

	E	F	G	H	
A					17
B					15
C					13
D					15
	15	2	16	27	

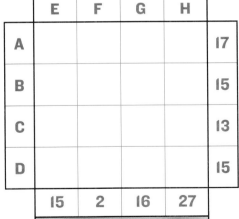

Across: D

DOWN

E
- Reggie Jackson's retired Yankees number
- Size of a full roster on an MLB team

F
- Year the Yankees last won the World Series

G
- Times Brazil has won the FIFA World Cup
- NBA center's concern: ___-second violation
- One under par for 18 holes at St. Andrews Old Course

H
- Number worn by Jaromir Jagr
- Only number in an NFL team nickname

BULKED-UP CROSSWORDS THAT DOUBLE THE ACTION

12-Across

ACROSS

1 Delhomme in Super Bowl XXXVIII
5 Broadcast deal, e.g.
9 Temple mascot
12 Two-time Super Bowl winner Roethlisberger
15 Mets G.M. Minaya
16 "___ sow, so shall..."
17 Brazilian Grand Prix city, for short
18 Pal for Tarzan
19 Leading Super Bowl receiver in almost every category
21 Blitzer's network
22 Tennis redo
23 Not turned up very high
24 Site of the first Super Bowl
27 HDTV maker
29 CFL and XFL centers?
30 Record-setting suffix
31 Lamar Hunt Trophy org.
34 "___ takers?"
36 ___ Strikes Out
38 Hike
42 Time when both hands are up
44 Buck and Aikman, e.g.
46 Tempe sch.
48 Requiem ___ a Heavyweight
49 Super Bowl victor with only one TD
53 Harness racing two-wheeler
55 Like the first Olympic competitors
56 One game ___ time
57 "Hey, over here" sound
58 NASCAR lids
60 Coach with 19 seasons between his only two Super Bowl appearances
64 Direct suffix
65 Honour given David Beckham (abbr.)
67 Always, in verse
68 Training ___
69 Wonderlic, e.g.
71 Super Bowl team for two cities
74 Rugby three-pointer
76 GI cops
77 Yoko from Tokyo
79 Admiral's or America's follower
81 Big fat mouth
83 Three-time Super Bowl MVP
87 Swimsuit model's asset
91 A League of Their ___
92 Racing surface for Joey Cheek
93 Coach with an 0–4 Super Bowl record
96 Meal for Sunday Silence
97 Groundskeeper's supply
98 Nike rival
99 K-___ (Andretti sponsor)
100 Org. Heston once headed
101 Serpentine route
102 Budweiser Clydesdale's harness
103 Some 35mm cameras, briefly

DOWN

1 Starbuck once married to Terry
2 Corner preceder at Augusta
3 Jazz great Malone
4 Cause of an unearned run, often
5 Duffer's goal
6 "___ live and breathe!"
7 Compete in a criterium
8 Start a round of golf
9 Quint's boat in Jaws
10 Half the Super Bowl participants
11 Defensive ends Howie and Chris
12 Super ___ (item that inspired the big game's name)
13 Modern pentathlon equipment
14 Jocks in Jersey jerseys
20 Rec center for girls
25 Denver to Dallas dir.
26 UFO pilots
28 Steffi's hubby
31 Curry of the Today show
32 Opponent
33 They've been in eight Super Bowls
35 Laugh syllable
37 Remote control batteries
39 Every Super Bowl contender since 1970
40 NASA's "thumbs up"
41 Be nosy
43 Long-distance swimmer Diana
45 Resort town near Santa Barbara
47 1984 Olympics boycotter
50 Approximately
51 And more, for short
52 ___ Down (wrestling film)
54 Mil. branch Trevino served in
57 William "The Refrigerator" ___
58 In the zone, as a shooter
59 Gold or silver, e.g.
60 Drug-busting org.
61 Longtime player
62 1992 Winter Olympics mascot: Magique the snow ___
63 CD forerunners
66 They lost a Super Bowl by 45 points
70 Landry with two Super Bowl titles
72 Longtime record label
73 Super Bowl ___
75 Harvard rival
78 Play-calling interference
80 Runner Nurmi who won nine Olympic golds
82 Ali's prefight compositions
83 Elway in five Super Bowls
84 Man ___ (horse racing great)
85 A Day Without Rain singer
86 Hendricks and Ginn Jr.
88 Track shape
89 Suns G.M. Steve
90 France-to-N.Y. fliers, once
94 NHL winger Antropov
95 Infamous Panther Carruth

83-Across

Give Me a Ring

ACROSS

1 *SI* model Refaeli
4 Dodger, to a disgruntled Brooklynite
7 *SI* model Alexis
10 *SI* model who hosts *America's Next Top Model*
15 Hole in one
16 Bob Gibson's was 1.12 in 1968
17 Lavatory, at the Grand National
18 Arabian ruler (var.)
19 *SI* model with a Kmart clothing line
21 Numero ___
22 *SI* model Cheryl
23 Brouhahas
24 Dog food brand
26 Gates's online service
27 Football's Amos Alonzo ___
29 Grammy-winning *SI* cover model
33 Frazier of the Knicks
36 Fill
38 NFL units
39 Sculling need
40 *100 Years...100 Movies* org.
41 RR stop
42 LBJ's successor
44 Russian *SI* model ___ V
45 *Harper's* ___ magazine
47 Skiing great Stenmark
50 *SI* model who hosted MTV's *House of Style*
52 *SI* model in *National Lampoon's Vacation*
56 Scores
58 Close-in baskets

59 Turn down
62 *Luck* ___ *Lady*
63 *SI* model Carol
64 Clamp shape
65 "___ had it up to here!"
66 ___ polloi
68 World Series component
70 Stadium level
71 *SI* model/race car driver
73 Dempsey's 1923 opponent
75 Two-time U.S. Open winner
76 Prefix meaning "ten"
78 Tehran resident
82 *SI* model Shayk
85 Golfer Sutton
86 Mexican *SI* cover model
88 More eerie
89 www.si.com, e.g.
90 Wimbledon do-over
91 Frasier's producer on *Frasier*
92 Charles Stengel, more familiarly
93 Masters creek eponym
94 *CBS Sports Spectacular* background music grp.
95 Pitched ___-hitter

DOWN

1 Artificial fly, e.g.
2 Bat prefix at the circus
3 Willis of the Knicks
4 "The ___ of the East"
5 Spigoted vessel
6 Amy of *Field of Dreams*
7 *SI* model who hosts *Project Runway*
8 Charged particles
9 Cow's call
10 The LPGA's King and Rawls
11 Protein-building acid
12 Evonne Cawley, ___ Goolagong
13 Beer bash barrel
14 Veteran H.S. players
20 Got beaten
25 Contract negotiator (abbr.)
26 Kind of school for docs
28 Houston team
29 Browns running back Earnest
30 ___-fat milk
31 Sixth of some six-packs
32 Before, in poetry
33 NYC's original *Monday Night Football* station
34 In the distance

1-Across

35 Actress/singer Minnelli
37 Northwest ending
41 Ump's call
43 Sporty British roadsters
44 Baseball great ___ Vaughan
46 Out of whack
47 Run in neutral
48 *SI* cover model Marisa
49 Vet sch. subject
51 Puzzle cube inventor
53 A daughter of Lyndon and Lady Bird
54 Tool for a duel
55 Strategic Belgian river of WWI
57 Ballfield putout
59 Down-and-up parallel bars move
60 *SI* model Herzigova
61 Goalie's back-up?
63 Friendly
66 *SI* model ___ Rhoda
67 Mil. training academy
69 2007 Pro Bowl winner
70 *SI* model Praver
72 *SI* model Simonsen
74 Ford with "horse" power
76 *SI* model/swimmer Torres
77 *SI* model Macpherson
79 Gillette razor
80 "___ Deion"
81 Spartans basketball coach Tom
82 Org. with a five-ring logo
83 Vitamin label amt.
84 Proofs of age
85 Chariot racer Judah Ben-___
87 Spearfisherman's catch

52-Across

Model
Citizens

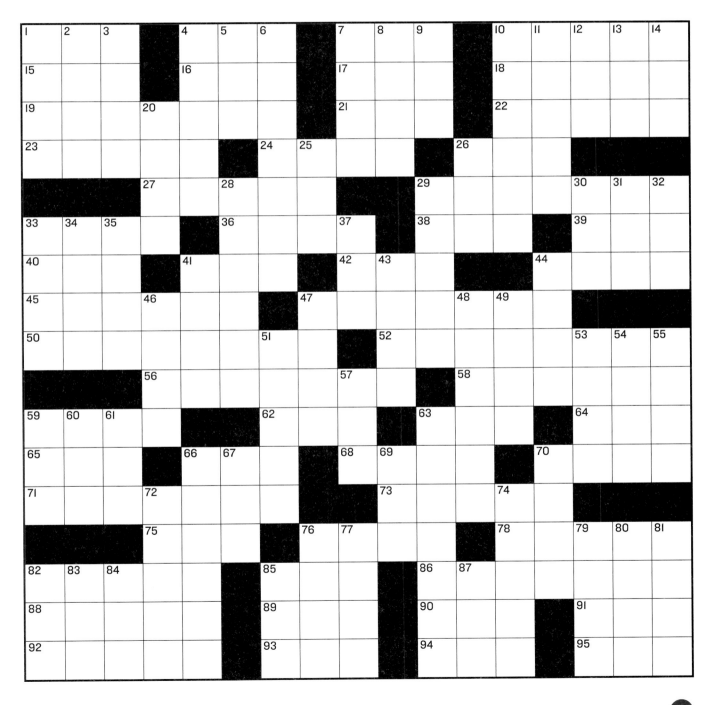

11-Down

ACROSS

1 Arena cupful, perhaps
5 Indent key
8 Sch. with 24 Tournament appearances and no Final Fours
11 Colorado ski resort
15 Dominant breed in endurance riding
16 Self-questioning question
17 MLB's Farmer and Figueroa
18 Cuba and Aruba (abbr.)
19 Nickname for the Tournament
22 Humdinger
23 Certain lodge member
24 Like high-turnover games
25 Family mem.
27 Engine covers
29 Damage
32 Converse ties
36 Out of control
38 The Final Four's Saturday games
40 Leading the pack
42 Shaq's Superman logo, e.g.
43 "My treat"
44 Hosp. helpers
45 Ties, as a match
47 Race, as an engine
49 Top four picks in the Tournament
51 Nickname for the Tournament
56 NFL pick
57 Mantle's number
58 "Is that true ___ lie?"
59 *A Day at the Races* name
62 Three-bagger
65 Speed, for a point guard, e.g.
67 Prelude to the Final Four
69 UCLA's Alcindor and others
70 Olympic parader with an all-green flag
71 A Stooge in *Three Little Pigskins*
72 Chocolate substitute
75 Second full day of the Tournament (abbr.)
77 Christopher of *Superman*
79 JFK airport alt.
82 Flag-dropping street vehicle
85 The Tournament's third round
89 Tournament title game winner by a record 30 pts. in 1990
90 Tiriac of tennis
91 Motorists org. that sanctioned Indy races through 1955
92 Mark raised on a pug's mug
93 One of two found 90 feet from home
94 Silent permission
95 4th yr. players
96 Vegas line

DOWN

1 "What he's having"
2 Type of contract
3 Long shot
4 *Wide World of Sports* network
5 No longer wild
6 Collect, as wins
7 Olympic site proposals
8 "War" of words
9 RB's stat
10 "Miracle on Ice" ctry.
11 No. 8 seed tournament winner
12 The Sun Devils' sch.
13 "Fighting" team, on a scoreboard
14 Big Baby's 2006 Final Four team
20 Grp. with a co-pay
21 The Amazins
26 Marrero or Manning
28 Approves
30 Tkt. price, e.g.
31 Brazilian hot spot
33 Sink, as a jump shot
34 Fairway overhanger, perhaps
35 NNW about-face
36 Ben Wallace 'do, sometimes
37 The Golden Gophers state (abbr.)
38 Diego and Francisco intros
39 ___ ahead (drive on)
41 Many an Olympic gymnast
42 "Splendid Splinter" Williams
46 Le Mans-winning Chevy, familiarly
48 Writer Ferber or Buchanan
50 Starting complement for the Tournament
51 Black tie in taekwondo
52 "Now ___ seen everything!"
53 ___ section (cheap seats)
54 Scull sport
55 Has a burger, e.g.
57 Basketball, e.g.
59 Stottlemyre of baseball
60 "Thrilla in Manila" victor
61 One protected by a flak jacket
63 It's 10 feet above a lane
64 "May ___ now?"
66 ___-mo replay
68 Type of hole in a football helmet
72 Boxer Julio ___ Chavez
73 Popular athletic shoes
74 Ex-Bear Grossman
76 Gets an invite to the Tournament
78 DC-10 due-in times, briefly
80 Neuter, as a horse
81 Black or red pests
82 Hot ___
83 "Gimme ___!" (frequent Crimson Tide request)
84 Big sizes, briefly
86 Recruit, as a top player
87 Dwight Freeney, for one
88 Inside-the-arc bucket

14-Down

Rules of "The Road"

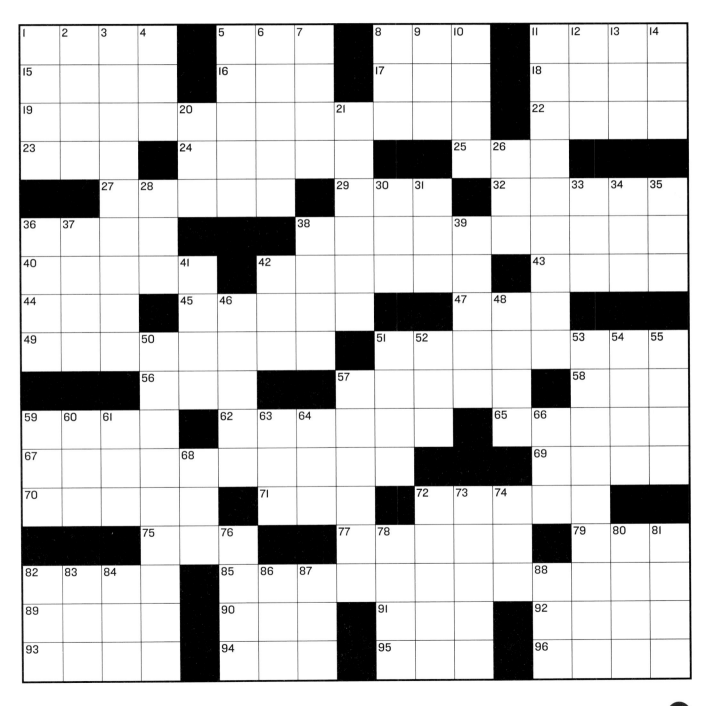

ACROSS

1 Sportscaster Barber
4 Hard-to-reach tennis return
7 Tie
11 Monopoly quartet (abbr.)
14 Killer serve
15 *SI* swimsuit model ___ Paula Araujo
16 The ___ Bowl in Aloha Stadium
17 Outscore
18 Sportscaster who told it like it was
21 "I've fallen ___ can't get up!"
22 Disinfectant brand
23 Like Birdie Kim or Grace Park
25 Funny ___ (racehorse)
28 "Oh my!" sportscaster
32 Albert E. Gator's college
36 Big name in tractors
37 Quarter of a quarter mile relay
38 See 55-Down
40 Triple jump parts
45 Sportscaster who announced elevator races on Letterman
46 Surfing need
47 Sportscaster who voiced "The thrill of victory... and the agony of defeat"
50 Final Four play-by-play man
54 Golfer Aoki
55 Skating analyst alongside Fleming
56 Sportscaster Musburger
58 Brian who won gold at the Calgary Olympics
60 Swish impediment
63 Lagoon formation
65 "Shame on you!" sounds
67 "Do you believe in miracles?" sportscaster
72 Got ___ from the judges
73 Fencing cry
74 Golfing great Walter
78 Jazzy James
79 "Whoa, Nellie!" sportscaster
86 Memo heading
87 Not playing
88 Common oar wood
89 Employ
90 Book ed.'s pile
91 Durham school
92 Oarsman's fraternity letter?
93 Tennis sportscaster Collins

DOWN

1 Pep rally shout
2 "Green" prefix
3 ___ Action Sports Tour
4 Golf sportscaster McCord
5 Concludes
6 Boise State's ___ Bell Arena
7 The NL doesn't allow them
8 Regret
9 The ___-Madden team
10 USFL Heisman winner
11 Zellweger of *Jerry Maguire*
12 JUGS gun technology
13 Charlotte's WNBA team
17 Fishhook feature
19 Ranger or Ray
20 Connie "Grand___ Man" Mack
24 Pair on Big Z's Cavaliers jersey
25 Grey Cup sports org.
26 Project suffix
27 Iditarod runner
29 Fateful March day
30 Road Runner frame
31 Nickelodeon's *Kenan & ___*
33 Camaro ___-Z
34 When many golf tournaments conclude
35 *The Thin Man* pooch
39 Willie "___ Hey" Mays
41 Skating champ Michelle
42 Golfer Baker-Finch
43 Sgt.'s charge
44 *Simon ___* (Dennis Rodman movie)
45 "Move it!"
47 Forward sail
48 Tennis player Shahar Pe'er's ctry.
49 Fannie ___
50 Stick out
51 "Let's just leave ___ that"
52 Super G sites (abbr.)
53 Cozy corner
55 With 38-Across, NBA legend who worked briefly as a commentator
57 RPM indicator
58 Feathery neckwear for Dennis Rodman
59 World Cup cheer
60 Q-U fillers
61 Steelers DB Taylor
62 AOL competitor
64 Nickname for Ted Williams
66 Ethanol holder at Indy
67 First-stringers
68 Safety Ronnie and others
69 Westminster rejects
70 "___ hardly wait!"
71 "Quiet!"
75 Slightly open
76 Ugly boxing wound
77 Repeat
80 Coll. website ender
81 Sort
82 Target in curling
83 Player off the bench
84 Woody Hayes sch.
85 Homer and Marge's neighbor

79-Across

18-Across

Fine Ones
To Talk

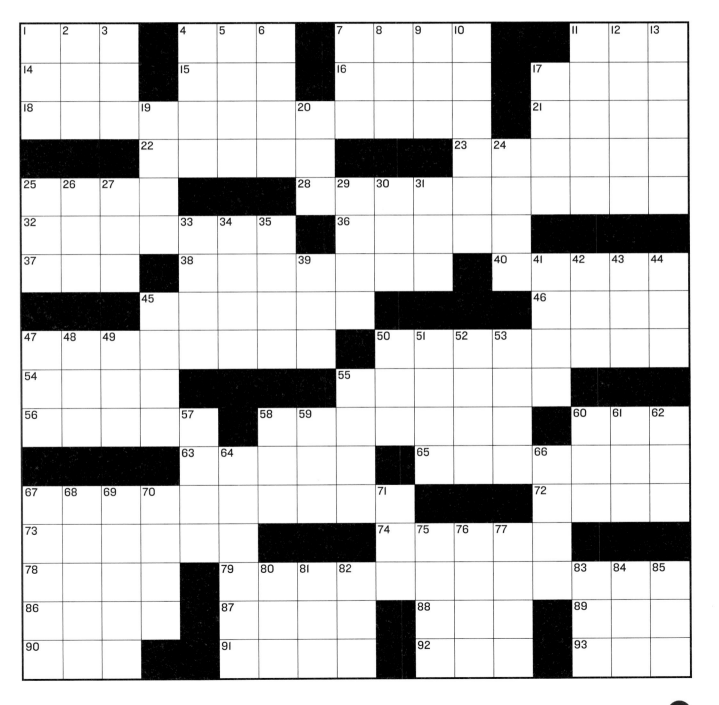

64-Across

ACROSS

1 Shriver with 112 doubles titles
4 Smallish batteries
7 Numerical endings
11 ___ Creek (Masters landmark)
15 Opening between the trees, e.g.
16 Title suffix for golfers
17 Come in third
18 Witty Bombeck
19 With 25-Across, site of the Masters
21 *Daytona USA* arcade game maker
22 ___-*Pro* (Will Ferrell movie)
23 Pebble Beach co-owner Eastwood
25 See 19-Across
27 Where Masters winners are
   interviewed at tournament's end
31 It's bent on Masters greens
32 Birthplace of many LPGA players
33 Modern ___
34 "I ___ next" (waiting player's call)
35 Guy's counterpart
36 *When It ___ a Game*
38 Site of Peru's Estadio Monumental
41 No, to Sandy Lyle
44 Scratch or dent
45 Youngest Masters champ
48 Info in a caddie's notebook
52 In position for a Masters win?
53 11-12-13 at the Masters
55 NYC subway line
56 Cricket hitter
57 Defensive back Ronnie
58 Bronzed
59 *Flags of ___ Fathers*
62 *Pat ___ Mike*
64 Birdie score on 16 at the Masters
66 Tiny Archibald
67 First Masters champ Horton ___

70 Masters champ symbol
74 Oldest Masters champ
76 Saints in the '08 and '09
   NCAA basketball tournament
77 R.E.M.'s *The ___ Love*
78 Masters champ Ballesteros
80 State for 19/25-Across
84 Jockey's strap
85 Sugar amts.
86 24 follower at Le Mans (abbr.)
87 Coxswain's lack
88 Monster truck amounts
89 "___ miracle!"
90 Doubled, an African fly
91 Prov. for the Blue Jays

DOWN

1 Tour involved in the Masters
2 The ___ James E. Sullivan Award
   (first won by Bobby Jones)
3 Car stat
4 Certain seat locale
5 Full of activity
6 Golfers' positions
7 Start for Snead or Stadler?
8 "Oh, yeah? ___ quit!"
9 ___ Bridge (Masters landmark)
10 The Sultan of ___
11 Doral Golf ___ & Spa
12 Boston Garden or
   Memorial Coliseum
13 Actresses Samms and Thompson
14 They're rigged at regattas
20 Bruins' sch.
24 Paving material
26 "Where did ___ wrong?"
27 Caddie's burden
28 Common Olympics chant
29 "It ain't over ___ it's over"

30 Hope/Crosby "Road" destination
34 Golfer Sergio
36 Female WWII grp.
37 Masters champ Palmer
39 Tennis's Kunitsyn or Andreev
40 All of 19/25-Across's members,
   controversially
41 Neither's partner
42 There are few of them
   during Masters telecasts
43 Japan or Taiwan suffix
44 Type of bike used off-road (abbr.)
45 Camp shelter
46 Dog-eared
47 Word after "9" on a golf scorecard
48 Apply, as lotion
49 Sam & Dave chorus: "___ Soul Man"
50 14 golf clubs, e.g.
51 ___-Magnon
54 Major ending for a baton twirler
58 ESPN's *Baseball ___*
59 The Big ___ Tree (Masters landmark)
60 Salt Lake City player
61 No longer playing (abbr.)
62 Pro Football Hall-of-Famer Doug
63 Org. with some masked players
65 Bullets star Unseld
66 The Tar Heels sch.
67 Emulate a bull
68 Actor Sal of *Somebody
   Up There Likes Me*
69 Strand, as an Arctic ship
70 Nonmember at a club
71 Replies to an invitation
72 Bleacher boos, e.g.
73 Win by ___
75 ___ Spumante wine
79 Tikkanen of hockey
81 Muck
82 Masters champ Woosnam
83 Masters champ Wall Jr.

74-Across

Masters of the Universe

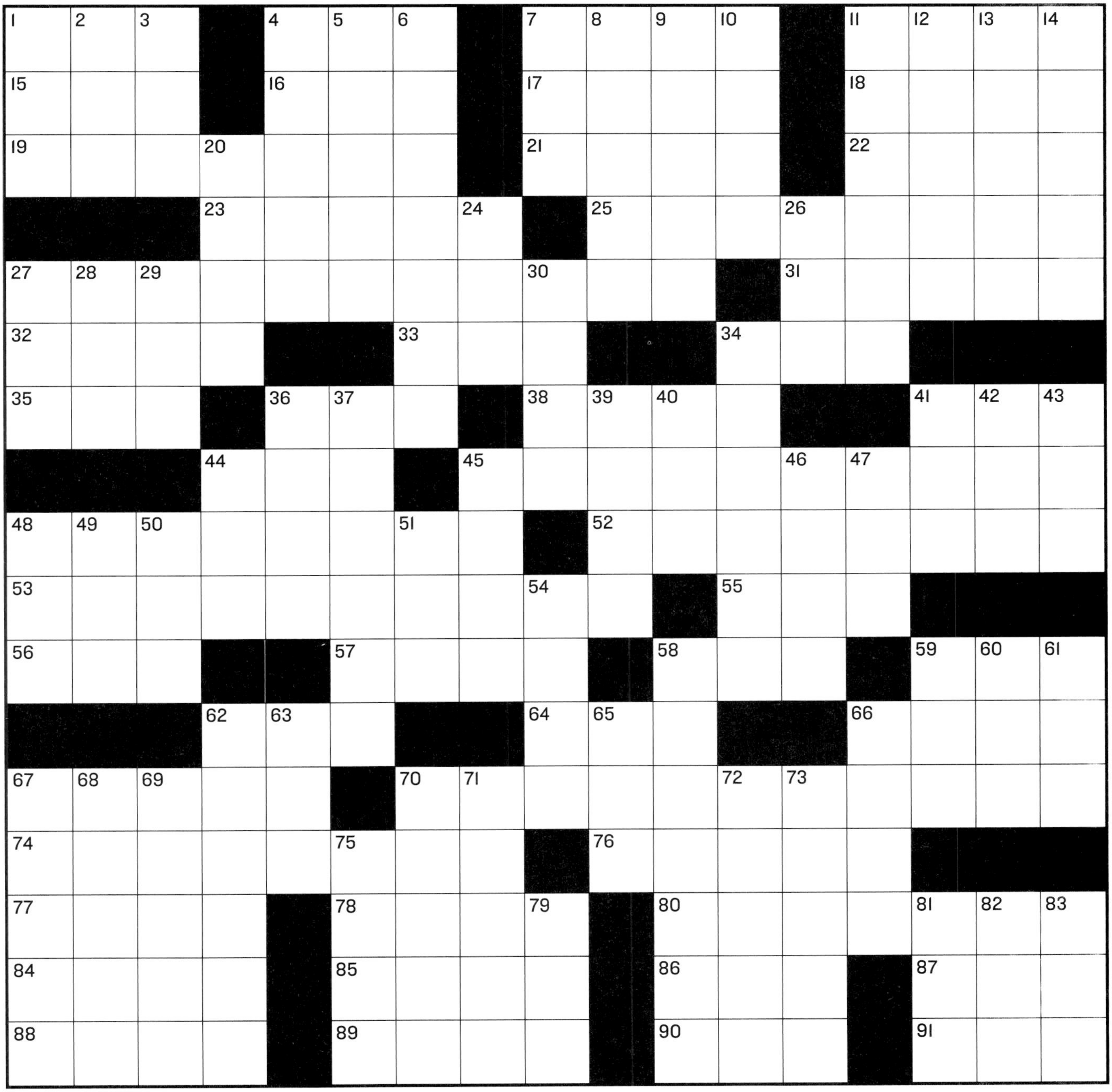
1
2
3
4
5
6
7
8
9
10
11
12
13
14
15
16
17
18
19
20
21
22
23
24
25
26
27
28
29
30
31
32
33
34
35
36
37
38
39
40
41
42
43
44
45
46
47
48
49
50
51
52
53
54
55
56
57
58
59
60
61
62
63
64
65
66
67
68
69
70
71
72
73
74
75
76
77
78
79
80
81
82
83
84
85
86
87
88
89
90
91

ACROSS

1 "___ on first?"
5 "You couldn't ___ more of them"
8 ___ Missouri
11 Snapshot
14 Foul on the arm, in b-ball
15 "Do or ___"
16 "Put up or ___ up"
17 Hall-of-Famer Gehrig
18 Italian wine region
19 The Matterhorn, for one
20 Knocks it in from off the green
22 "Ouch!"
25 Miner's find
26 Prince Valiant's son
27 Ships in Space Jam
31 "Everyone contributed"
37 "___ matter of fact..."
38 By way of
39 The Stanford ___ (Big Game trophy)
40 Many Heisman winners (abbr.)
41 Stadium topper
43 Biondi or Hasselbeck
44 College sports org.
46 NFL fan's "hold 'em" rebus sign
48 "And the stadium ___!"
52 Pointed swan dive parts
54 Olympic sprinter Devers
57 Manhattan shopping neighborhood
58 Nose about
61 Downhill race sites (abbr.)
62 Lessen, as momentum
63 Big Johns Hopkins sport, familiarly
64 "It's now or never"
70 Type of cycling helmet
71 Gun, at a drag race
72 BlackBerry, for one

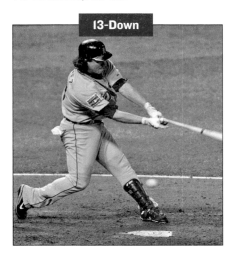

13-Down

73 "Don't look ahead"
81 Vehicle that carries drivers in the back
84 Tire-inflating unit (abbr.)
85 Revered superstar
86 Nile snake
87 "___ is like kissing your sister"
88 Olympic sprint medalist Boldon
89 2000 Olympic women's basketball coach Fortner
90 "Warm up the ___"
91 Trio before UV
92 Cheated while racewalking
93 Racehorse's starting spot

DOWN

1 "That's ___ great players do"
2 Type of gridiron mark
3 Prefix meaning "eight"
4 Lift for downhillers
5 Clichés
6 Farm structure
7 Didn't quit
8 "This can't be good"
9 Star Trek helmsman
10 Hoop or drag add-on
11 Arafat's org.
12 Short poker player's slip
13 "Good ___!"
16 Poker spokesmodel Hiatt
21 Double ___ Oreos
23 Span. woman
24 "Watching them play is a ___"
28 "Go ___ broke"
29 Golf or squash ball, e.g.
30 The U.S.A.'s 50 (abbr.)
31 "If this ___ any help..."

22-Across

32 Subdue, as an opponent
33 Gardner of On the Beach
34 "You da ___!"
35 Stand out
36 "They strike ___ in the hearts of their opponents"
37 "If I might ___..."
42 Lord of the Rings bad guy
43 "Where rubber ___ the road"
45 2000 Olympics host ctry.
47 "They've ___ to play"
49 Sport with chukkers
50 Winter Olympics worry
51 White or Red follower
53 Nine-digit ID
54 "Let's go ___!"
55 Like bad golf scores
56 Office machine co.
58 School org.
59 Baseball scoreboard trio
60 The Stones' Get ___ Ya-Ya's Out!
65 Raise the ___
66 Give a halftime speech, e.g.
67 Play that might involve a pitch
68 Nutrition fig.
69 102.9, e.g., for a quarterback
74 MJ's alma mater
75 Takes, as a loss
76 Stick-to-it-iveness
77 Dog in The Thin Man
78 "What's the big ___?"
79 Shed feathers
80 First name of a five-time SI cover model
81 Chat
82 Sch. with six Heisman winners
83 CD forerunners

You Can Say That Again

11-Down

ACROSS

1 Type of center or room
4 Sixth sense
7 Sauna sites
11 No. 1 NBA pick Daugherty ('86)
15 Stat rarely below 2.00
16 No. 1 NBA pick Heyman ('63)
17 2001 World Series MVP Schilling
18 No. 1 NBA pick ('08)
19 African home of two No. 1 NBA picks
21 ___ in a Lifetime
22 "___ boy!"
23 No. 1 NBA pick out of LSU ('92)
24 Only college to have consecutive No. 1 NFL picks, familiarly
27 Concepción or Bench, notably
29 Was behind
30 Drench
33 Use up, as the clock
35 Morn's opposite
36 College of No. 1 NFL pick Eli Manning: ___ Miss ('04)
39 First No. 1 NBA pick directly out of high school ('01)
44 Restrained a racehorse, with "in"
46 Pro-Bowler Romo's full first name
47 Brick mason's carrier
49 Cleanup hitter's stat
50 Canon endorsed by Agassi
51 No. 1 NFL pick Emtman ('92) or Bartkowski ('75)
53 ___ Schwarz
54 No. 1 NBA pick Austin ('71) or No. 1 NFL pick David ('02)
56 Many, many moons
57 College of No. 1 NFL pick Harry Gilmer ('48)
61 No. 1 NFL pick Davis, formally ('62)
64 Home of the Ironmen who made the first ever No. 1 NBA pick ('47)
66 Third baseman Gómez
67 Like the torch during the Olympics
69 "So that's it!"
70 Positions for No. 1 NFL pick Gary Glick ('56) and others (abbr.)
71 Athlete at No. 1 NBA pick James Worthy's alma mater ('82)
74 No. 1 NBA pick Duncan ('97) or No. 1 NFL pick Couch ('99)
77 About one in three No. 1 NFL picks
81 "The ___" (Redskins receiving trio)
85 Sch. for No. 1 NBA pick Robinson ('87)
86 Groups of rioters
87 Tallest No. 1 NBA pick ('02)
89 NASCAR on Fox: Crank ___
90 Work without ___ (take risks)
91 Hat, informally
92 "O Sole ___"
93 Body art, slangily
94 MLB's Yost and others
95 6'3" South African golfer
96 Ave. crossers

DOWN

1 National Bowling Stadium city
2 Chicago Sky guard Thorn
3 Batting practice structure
4 Baseball Hall-of-Famer Combs
5 ___ Lanka
6 Orgs. that might raise funds with a student/faculty game
7 Search high and low
8 ___ football (emulate Jeff Feagles)
9 Father of two No. 1 NFL picks
10 Bradshaw, after being picked No. 1 in the NFL draft ('70)
11 No. 1 NBA pick out of Duke ('99)
12 On-campus mil. org.
13 Nick and Nora's dog
14 "Shuffle up and ___"
20 Pricked one at the Preakness
25 Football Hall-of-Famer Graham
26 Tennis great Lacoste
28 Figure skater Thomas
30 Jamaican music
31 Dominate, in sports lingo
32 College coach of No. 1 NFL pick Ki-Jana Carter ('95)
34 Came up
36 Type of NASCAR race camera
37 Pipeline Masters winner's neckwear
38 No. 1 NFL pick "Too Tall" Jones ('74) and others
40 007 portrayer Roger
41 85-Across grad's rank (abbr.)
42 The Pussycat Dolls' ___ Grow Up
43 NBA season's first full mo.
45 Yankee pitcher Hideki ___
48 Sudden ___
52 ___ Rank Boxing
53 Collegiate adjective for No. 1 NBA pick Chris Webber ('93)
54 Animation frame
55 We ___ Marshall
58 Exam for a future atty.
59 Classic British sports car
60 Sounds made during a physical
62 Bed support
63 Pit crew member who changes rubber
65 Sprinkle for Minnesota Fats
68 King's chair
71 Clay pigeon hurlers
72 Dwindled, as fan interest
73 Divisions for the Orioles and Braves
75 Apple players
76 "Hi, ___" (shout to a TV camera)
77 Throw in the towel
78 Davis Cup org.
79 "Sometimes you feel like ___..."
80 No. 1 NFL pick Rote ('51)
82 No. 1 NFL pick Billy ('80)
83 Temper tantrum
84 Some No. 1 picks have big ones
88 Hurt

82-Down

We're
Number One!

ACROSS

1 Round-trippers (abbr.)
4 He trails only Wilt for most points in a game
8 ___ American Games
11 *Chariots of* ___
15 Lamprey, e.g.
16 Tons
17 Angelina Jolie model role
18 Can't miss a shot
19 George Clooney football movie
22 Bankroll
23 *Field of Dreams* line: "___ build it, he will come"
24 Mets manager between Salty and Yogi
25 Egyptian boy king, for short
27 St. Louis to Chicago direction
29 Bill Murray golf comedy
35 Villanova's conference
39 *Rocky* ___
40 Took ___ (stood behind center)
41 Blind ___ bat
42 Tom Cruise in *Days of* ___
45 Stat for an NFL vet
46 *Bad News Bears* actress O'Neal
49 ___ *in a Million: The Ron LeFlore Story*
50 Player with a horseshoe on his helmet
53 Gene Hackman basketball movie
55 Paul Newman hockey movie
59 ___ *Sports with Bryant Gumbel*
60 Jean-Claude Killy's "yes"
61 Witticisms
62 Jason played him in *Rudy*
64 *Damn* ___

68 Actress Peeples or Vardalos
69 Cuba Gooding Jr. football movie
72 Sailor's "Help!"
73 Power hitter
76 Robert Redford baseball movie
79 Sugar suffix
80 Nickname for runner Steve
81 ___-trick (three goals by one player, if scored consecutively)
83 In any way
87 *SI* model Brinkley's ex
90 Cycling movie featuring "The Cutters"
94 "In the ___" (intentional grounding phrase)
95 Morsel in *Seabiscuit*
96 Lake that can be seen from Cleveland Stadium
97 NBA conference suffix
98 Movie with a Brett Favre cameo: *There's Something About* ___
99 Welker of the Patriots
100 Units in *Pumping Iron*
101 *Semi-Tough* author Jenkins

DOWN

1 Port or pad lead-in
2 *Blue Crush* danger
3 Defeat
4 "Big ___" (top surfer in *Beach Blanket Bingo*)
5 Bullfight chant
6 Björn of tennis
7 Has a strong work ___
8 The Players Championship org.
9 First ___ station
10 Ilie's tennis nickname
11 So-so finishes
12 Terre Haute sch.
13 Heisman winner Dayne
14 Film's climax
20 Muscle quality
21 Julia's role on *Seinfeld*
26 *Miracle on Ice* chant
28 Long or short add-on
30 Performed, as a routine
31 *Surf Nazis Must* ___
32 ___ goes (no holds barred)
33 Herbie in *Herbie: Fully Loaded*, e.g.
34 G.I. mess duties
35 English rugby club of note
36 Aoki on the Champions Tour

29-Across

37 University of Florida drink
38 Explorer Heyerdahl
43 Young '___ (tykes)
44 ___ Dome (Former Colts stadium)
47 ___ the glass (bank it)
48 Soccer's Hamm
51 Trio following N
52 The Southeastern Conf. Tigers
54 NBA center-forward Melvin
55 Take to court
56 Rough situations?
57 Mayberry boy
58 Old Russian ruler
60 Olympian Baiul
62 Receiver Monk
63 Stadium shout
65 Sparky the Sun Devil's sch.
66 38-Down's ctry.
67 ___-mo
70 Not out-of-bounds
71 Regatta trophy
74 Customary practices
75 ___ ruling (consult course officials)
77 2007 Heisman winner Tim
78 What Fletch imagines himself to be in *Fletch*
82 Roller in *Talladega Nights*
84 Wowed
85 ___ *Croft: Tomb Raider*
86 Swann in *The Waterboy*
87 *Space* ___ (Michael Jordan movie)
88 "...boy ___ girl?"
89 Ballad or musket suffix
91 ___ Dawn Chong of *American Flyers*
92 *The X-Files* subj.
93 ___ at the finish line (barely beat)

11-Across

Screen Passes

52-Across

ACROSS

1 Prep for a fight
5 Tour de France peaks
9 Equestrian doc
12 "The Penguin" at third
15 The "P" in UTEP
16 The NFL's Junior ___
17 Home of Gaelic football (abbr.)
18 Strings for Tiny Tim
19 Only team to win more than one Series in two different cities
21 Team that lost the first Series
23 Length of DiMaggio's hit streak, in Roman numerals
24 MPG-rating org.
26 Unit for an Olympic wrestler
27 More risqué
30 Wide out
32 "You want a piece ___?!"
35 Oscars host DeGeneres
36 Pitcher with a record 23 strikeouts in a four-game Series
40 Bali ___ (South Pacific song)
41 Poker phrase while mucking
43 Batting helmet's ____ hole
44 Longtime logo on Petty's #43
45 Air rifle supply
47 They're often downed at dart matches
48 Thompson of All the Right Moves
50 Only manager to be ejected from two Series games
52 Last of the original teams of 1903 to win a Series (they did it in 1980)

57 ___ alai
58 Knocked in ___
59 About 2/5 of an average baseball field
60 Asset for Series MVP Whitey Ford
63 Genetic material
65 Earring sites
67 Notre Dame's "Era of ___" (1964–74)
68 Team in four of the first seven Series
71 Ohio home of the Pros (1920 football champs)
73 Game-winning home run hitter, e.g.
74 Basinger of The Natural
75 Steinbrenner and Reinsdorf, for two
76 The D-backs home
79 It's off on a wild pitch
81 102, in old Rome
82 Only nonpitcher to win the Series MVP twice
85 The first one in a World Series took place in 1971
90 Rice mascot ejected from a 2009 basketball game
91 Game outfit, for short
92 "Do ___ others..."
93 Swimmer Gary Jr. or Sr.
94 Wide width for a pair of cleats
95 Rally or squad preceder
96 Reliever José "Joe Table" ___
97 Bar bills

DOWN

1 Whirlpool bath
2 2008 Phillie Burrell
3 Louisville Slugger wood

4 1974 Series MVP Fingers
5 In motion
6 Hula Bowl neckwear
7 No. 1 NFL draft pick Orlando
8 Punishes for brawling, perhaps
9 Luxury box bigwig
10 Rally driver Carlsson
11 Hatcher of Desperate Housewives
12 Interceptions of throws to home
13 ___ out a victory
14 Marv Albert call
20 "___ could do that!"
22 Outfielder Moisés
25 "___...they're off!" (track announcer's line)
27 Postinjury program
28 The ___ Bowl in San Antonio
29 Take on K2, e.g.
31 Golf course designer Pete
33 Beam dismount surface
34 Milk carton abbr. preceding a date
36 Least productive homer variety
37 Third baseman Rodriguez
38 "Mr. Tiger" in the 1968 Series
39 1988 Series MVP Hershiser
42 Batting against
46 It commonly follows a verb (abbr.)
49 Univ. Joe Namath attended
51 Repeated Seinfeld word
52 "Not a ___!" ("No sweat!")
53 Wheel centers
54 "Hah! See if ___!"
55 The "E" of 61-Down
56 Infielders Casey and Berry
58 Softball bat material, often
60 Cry from Boris Becker
61 Ballpark scoreboard letters
62 1969 Mets adjective
64 "Good to go"
66 "You ___ here first"
69 Filling found in Sosa's bat, once
70 Spy org.
72 1986 World Series MVP Ray
75 Mexican golfer Lorena
77 Has left the on deck circle
78 Man-on-man alternative
80 Fly ball chaser's cry
82 "Say it ain't so, ___"
83 Amaze
84 Barely beat
86 Some race cars
87 Pacific Coast League, e.g.
88 Org. with one Canadian and 29 U.S. teams
89 Winner at Oakmont in 1994

The Boys of Autumn

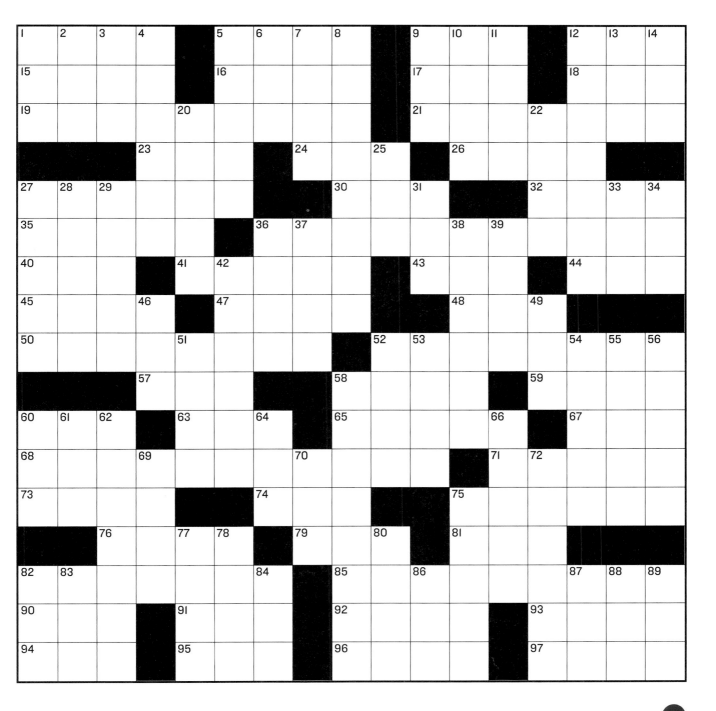

32-Across

ACROSS

1 *Hoosiers* or *The Warriors*
5 Outfield hit
8 Citi Field fielder
11 ___ the Niner (UNC mascot)
15 Stick ___ in the water
16 Two-time U.S. Open winner Janzen
17 Meter prefix
18 *NCAA Football*: rated ___ Everyone
19 Athletes at Gonzaga, Yale and over 30 other colleges
21 Long Beach State's baseball team (really!)
23 Backyard cookout spot
24 Athlete at Pace University
25 NHL or MLS, e.g.
27 Four-baggers (abbr.)
28 Pete and Penny, for Youngstown State's mascots
32 Athlete at Grambling, Missouri and over 20 other colleges
36 Nolan with 5,714 strikeouts
38 Average
39 2008 AL Rookie of the Year Longoria
40 It's covered by a headset
41 Athletes at Virginia Tech
43 Athletes at Arkansas
47 Went ___ road trip
48 Hero ending
49 Writer, briefly
50 Locker room bottleful
52 Pitcher Seaver
55 Bill Walton's position (abbr.)
56 Marshall's ___ Herd
59 Athlete
62 Lennon's widow
63 Winnebago owner, informally
64 Judge's seat
65 Links lag
66 TCU's Horned ___
67 Skater ___ Anton Ohno
69 Sue Grafton's ___ *for Alibi*
70 Subj. for immigrants
72 SU's team
74 Is ahead
78 Hawaii's "colorful" baseball team
81 Delaware's Fighting ___
84 Unit equaling roughly 90 yards of a football field
85 D.C. baseballer
86 ___ Jay (KU's mascot)
87 Future race in *The Time Machine*
88 West Point chow hall
89 Mock or crock ending
90 They take hikes, briefly
91 The Bryn ___ Owls

DOWN

1 "Groovy!"
2 Suck ___
3 *Damn Yankees* temptress
4 Become unsuitable for skiing
5 Press all the way, as an accelerator
6 Punter's "kicker"
7 "Do you believe in miracles? ___!"
8 The ___ pentathlon
9 Changes text
10 Civil wrong
11 The Cornhuskers school
12 "Son ___ gun!"
13 Baseball's Maris, to pals
14 ___ Wuf (N.C. State's female mascot)
20 Fashion designer Christian
22 Soccer star's number, traditionally
24 "Man-eating" athlete at Nova Southeastern
26 Albany's ___ Danes
29 "Me!?"
30 DePaul-to-Pitt dir.
31 *Titanic* message
32 Garr of *Young Frankenstein*
33 Shortstop DeJesús
34 Look at the stars
35 David Bowie collaborator Brian
37 America's Cup entry
41 Stop on 3rd down
42 How many times CCNY has won the NCAA basketball championship
44 Assess, as a prospect
45 Raymond of *Perry Mason*
46 Cheerleading feat
51 Make ___ of (jot down)
52 Set-top box with instant replay
53 A thou
54 Connie Mack and Tony La Russa (abbr.)
55 Athletes at Iowa State
57 "The ___ That Ruth Built"
58 Basics of education initials
59 Org. for Earl Anthony
60 *Phar* ___
61 "It's ___-brainer"
65 Oinker's abode
66 Escape
68 Sphere
69 Egypt's Sadat
71 UC-Santa Cruz's Banana ___
73 Blue-ribbon
75 Throat-clearing sound
76 Oscar ___ Hoya
77 Ski jump need
78 Athlete at Colorado State or Fordham
79 Purple ___ (Evansville athlete)
80 Tax org.
81 Tailgate cookout, briefly
82 Ad ___
83 Title for Edmund Hillary

43-Across

What's in a Nickname?

UNDER REV

CAN YOU SPOT THE DIFFERENCES?

(Don't worry, it gets harder!)

The Long Run

Pittsburgh linebacker James Harrison needs a moment after his 100-yard interception return against Arizona in Super Bowl XLIII.

Look for **8** differences

**Check them off
as you find them** ◯ ◯ ◯ ◯ ◯ ◯ ◯ ◯

Track Meat

Standing in the way of tradition can get rocky, as Colorado's
Paul Phillips learned at the sixth-inning sausage race in Milwaukee.

Look for **10** differences

Check them off as you find them ◯ ◯ ◯ ◯ ◯ ◯ ◯ ◯ ◯ ◯

Into the Blue

Danny Green maintained his calm amid the Cameron Crazies
in this 2008 meeting between Duke and North Carolina.

Look for **10** differences

Check them off as you find them ◯ ◯ ◯ ◯ ◯ ◯ ◯ ◯ ◯ ◯

Passing Lanes

The traffic was heavy, but moving quickly, as college teammates
made the baton handoff at the 2004 Penn Relays.

Look for 10 differences

Check them off as you find them ◯ ◯ ◯ ◯ ◯ ◯ ◯ ◯ ◯ ◯

Over and Out

White Sox fans had a better shot than the Tigers' Clete Thomas
at grabbing this 2009 A.J. Pierzynski home run.

Look for 9 differences

Check them off as you find them ○ ○ ○ ○ ○ ○ ○ ○ ○

Prepare for Landing

Even this Olympic equestrian rider had to steel herself for impact
after her horse made a big jump at Beijing.

Look for ⑩ differences

Check them off as you find them ◯ ◯ ◯ ◯ ◯ ◯ ◯ ◯ ◯ ◯

High and Mighty

As his drive to the hoop shows, Dayton's London Warren was clearly up for this January 2008 game against Xavier.

Look for 10 differences

Check them off as you find them ○ ○ ○ ○ ○ ○ ○ ○ ○ ○

A Posing Force

Detroit celebrates winning the Stanley Cup on enemy ice in Pittsburgh in 2008—a favor the Penguins would return in 2009.

Look for ⑩ differences

Check them off as you find them ◯ ◯ ◯ ◯ ◯ ◯ ◯ ◯ ◯ ◯

Prime Interest

With the spotlight on him at media day for Super Bowl XXIX
in Miami, Deion Sanders knew enough to wear shades.

Look for **8** differences

Check them off as you find them ◯ ◯ ◯ ◯ ◯ ◯ ◯ ◯

Running Out of Water

The Ming Tomb Reservoir made a striking setting for the swimming leg of the women's triathlon at the Beijing Olympics.

Look for 8 differences

**Check them off
as you find them** ○ ○ ○ ○ ○ ○ ○ ○

Big Easy Reading

The souvenir newspapers told the story when LSU defeated
Ohio State for the BCS championship in New Orleans in 2008.

Look for **9** differences

Check them off as you find them ○ ○ ○ ○ ○ ○ ○ ○ ○

Legging It Out

Cornell's John Glynn gets out from in-between against
Syracuse at the 2009 NCAA lacrosse championship.

Look for ⑩ differences

**Check them off
as you find them** ◯◯◯◯◯◯◯◯◯◯

Boom Time

Mark McGwire's 70th long ball capped the 1998 home run race—a historic moment that, it turned out, was not quite all that it seemed.

Look for **8** differences

Check them off as you find them ◯ ◯ ◯ ◯ ◯ ◯ ◯ ◯

Mogul Mayhem

Talk about a stiff upper flip! A female skier begins a freestyle run
at the 2006 Winter Games in Torino.

Look for **8** differences

Check them off as you find them ○ ○ ○ ○ ○ ○ ○ ○

Quick Change Artists

When Jimmie Johnson pulls in for a pit stop, as he did here
at Martinsville, his crew becomes a blue streak.

Look for **8** differences

Check them off as you find them ◯ ◯ ◯ ◯ ◯ ◯ ◯ ◯

The Green Party

Packers tight end Donald Lee feels the love after making the
Lambeau Leap following a touchdown in 2007.

Look for ⑨ differences

Check them off as you find them ◯ ◯ ◯ ◯ ◯ ◯ ◯ ◯ ◯

Dish Network

An over-the-shoulder glance was all Kobe Bryant needed to find teammate Trevor Ariza in this 2009 playoff series against Houston.

Look for **9** differences

Check them off as you find them ◯ ◯ ◯ ◯ ◯ ◯ ◯ ◯ ◯

Crash Scene

The Brewers' Prince Fielder got past Giants catcher Todd Greene,
but Corey Koskie was tagged by pitcher Brad Hennessey.

Look for ⑧ differences

**Check them off
as you find them** ◯ ◯ ◯ ◯ ◯ ◯ ◯ ◯

Golden Moment

His quest for eight gold medals at the 2008 Olympics completed,
Michael Phelps hugs his mother, Debbie.

Look for ⑩ differences

Check them off as you find them ○ ○ ○ ○ ○ ○ ○ ○ ○ ○

ANSWERS

STARTERS

Tiger Woods — Page 6

```
KFC . CPA . APPLY
NIA . HIS . THREE
ELDRICK . WOODS
EASY . AFOOT .
. ARBOR . ONJV
STANFORD . EEE
KIOSK . USHER
EEK . REDSHIRT
EDIE . EVENA .
. LTCOL . FLOP
STEVE . KULTIDA
TAPIN . EGO . EDS
PRANK . SET . SSS
```

Derek Jeter — Page 8

```
ACE . GRIT . HRS
BANG . HIGH . AFT
USER . ICERINKS
DEREKJETER .
YOGI . EVADE
. LAST . IRON
NEWYORKYANKEE
ILIE . MISS .
BYLAW . KOBE
. SHORTSTOPS
OLDTIMER . ITSA
ROO . TAPE . SCOT
RUN . ERSE . HMS
```

Tony Romo — Page 10

```
MAT . ERS . PROS
OPEN . GAP . LENT
TONYROMO . AXEL
ATSEA . STAY .
. RGS . BOCCE
ATS . UNDRAFTED
LEEJ . AYE . FROG
FREEAGENT . SSE
APASS . OHS .
. SUMO . AINGE
SEMI . ILLINOIS
ERIC . AGE . GULP
TADA . SAW . NAY
```

Chris Paul — Page 11

```
HIPS . SOSA . YOS
ONEK . INTL . ALA
CHRISPAUL . NET
HITTHE . PAK .
. SHOE . HORNETS
. WAKEFOREST
IRA . AMF . SPY
NEWORLEANS .
FIFTEEN . ITBE
. USS . INJARS
PAL . NBAROOKIE
GIL . ARLO . EEKA
AMY . PAIN . SRAS
```

John Madden — Page 12

```
GOLF . CAL . BUS
EMIL . SODA . ERE
ESPO . ERIN . AGE
. JOHNMADDEN
GOSOLO . ESE .
EVA . GRR . MSG
OAKLANDRAIDER
LEO . SOD . ANY
. LOO . YANKEE
HALLOFFAME .
OLE . HAIL . ESPN
CBS . EGGS . LEAN
HAS . DES . YALE
```

Rafael Nadal — Page 14

```
EPIC . JVS . RACE
REDO . III . ARUN
REEF . BAG . NERD
. RAFAELNADAL
. IDS . ANO .
STONE . OLYMPIC
PAL . MRS . ICU
FEDERER . OCTET
. JAR . DOH .
FRENCHOPENS .
IROC . UAW . RAIN
BELT . RIN . YMCA
FEES . YRS . LEST
```

Danica Patrick — Page 16

```
DAD . PAM . BRENT
ABE . ARA . AARON
SELECTS . SCANT
HEIDI . KNEE .
. SFO . OSCARS
OWE . IRAN . ASIA
DANICAPATRICK
ODIN . NEMO . THE
REDDOG . ENS .
. ITEM . ETHEL
SARAH . GODADDY
SCENE . RAU . TIL
SUGAR . STP . VEE
```

Ichiro Suzuki — Page 18

```
FEM . ETH . TNT
ILYA . NEO . SHOO
JETS . FOURIRON
ICHIRO . SUZUKI
. FOR . ENE .
JOG . ACE . UNIT
INSIDETHEPARK
BEAM . CUP . GEO
. ODD . REF .
JACKIE . LEAGUE
EXYANKEE . ROMA
SLAY . EAR . MVPS
TEN . DPS . SST
```

Shaun White — Page 19

```
ICED . DEW . RED
SHAUN . AAA . AXE
SERBO . WRS . JIM
. FLYINGTOMATO
. WASH . HUE .
MAE . ERN . TEAMS
CNBC . AFC . TTOP
SABRE . LAW . LEA
. EBB . RIPA .
SNOWBOARDING .
TIP . EGG . OTTOS
UKE . TEE . WHITE
BEN . SYD . SCOT
```

Joe Paterno — Page 20

```
JOE . GAWK . AARP
ARC . ILIE . SLUR
YER . PENNSTATE
SLUMP . STERN .
. RED . SLOANS
PATERNO . ASLOW
ALA . AWS . DOA
MOIST . NITTANY
SULTAN . XII .
. GALES . GNATS
HEADCOACH . SAT
ANTI . NYET . SPA
IDEA . SALS . TEN
```

Wayne Gretzky — Page 22

```
PAWNS . ROG . YES
ECHOS . EAR . ALL
WAYNE . GRETZKY
ERIC . RICA .
EDMONTONOILER
. MEOW . EMU
CROSBY . UNKNOT
AAH . EPEE .
PHOENIXCOYOTE
. REMI . LUIS
ARTROSS . KINGS
LOU . NET . EMCEE
ING . STS . VEERS
```

LeBron James — Page 24

```
TYS . POPUP . DJS
AAH . IRISH . REP
CLEVELAND . IRE
SEMI . ASA . BSA
. UPENN . CABER
. UDO . LILY
. LEBRONJAMES
. AAAS . EAR .
ASSHE . GEENA
PAT . LOU . LIKE
ALE . CAVALIERS
SLR . BLARE . COT
TEN . SALSA . ENS
```

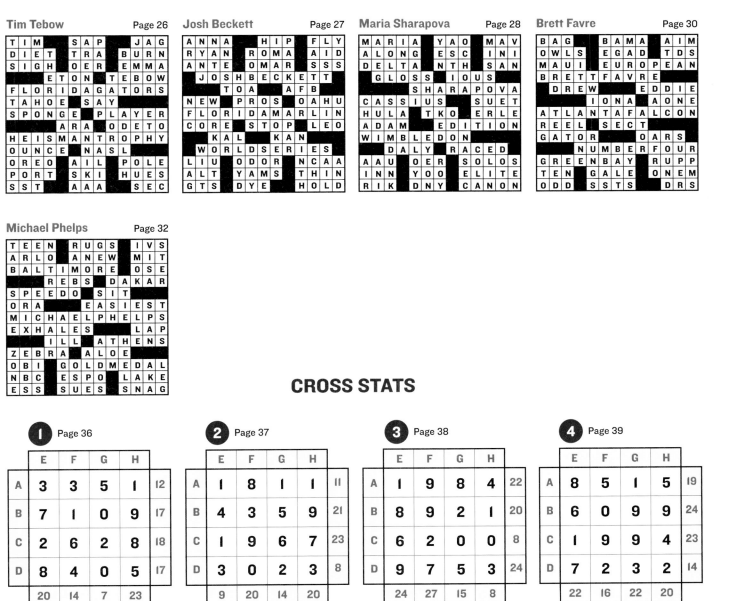

Tim Tebow — Page 26

T	I	M		S	A	P		J	A	G
D	I	E	T		T	R	A		B	U	R	N
S	I	G	H		O	E	R		E	M	M	A
		E	T	O	N		T	E	B	O	W
F	L	O	R	I	D	A	G	A	T	O	R	S
T	A	H	O	E		S	A	Y			
S	P	O	N	G	E		P	L	A	Y	E	R
		A	R	A		O	D	E	T	O	
H	E	I	S	M	A	N	T	R	O	P	H	Y
O	U	N	C	E		N	A	S	L		
O	R	E	O		A	I	L		P	O	L	E
P	O	R	T		S	K	I		H	U	E	S
S	S	T		A	A	A		S	E	C

Josh Beckett — Page 27

Crossword grid answers

Maria Sharapova — Page 28

Crossword grid answers

Brett Favre — Page 30

Crossword grid answers

Michael Phelps — Page 32

Crossword grid answers

CROSS STATS

1 — Page 36

	E	F	G	H	
A	3	3	5	1	12
B	7	1	0	9	17
C	2	6	2	8	18
D	8	4	0	5	17
	20	14	7	23

2 — Page 37

	E	F	G	H	
A	1	8	1	1	11
B	4	3	5	9	21
C	1	9	6	7	23
D	3	0	2	3	8
	9	20	14	20

3 — Page 38

	E	F	G	H	
A	1	9	8	4	22
B	8	9	2	1	20
C	6	2	0	0	8
D	9	7	5	3	24
	24	27	15	8

4 — Page 39

	E	F	G	H	
A	8	5	1	5	19
B	6	0	9	9	24
C	1	9	9	4	23
D	7	2	3	2	14
	22	16	22	20

5 — Page 39

	E	F	G	H	
A	9	1	3	2	15
B	2	0	0	0	2
C	4	0	8	1	13
D	6	7	5	2	20
	21	8	16	5

6 — Page 40

	E	F	G	H	
A	7	5	5	2	19
B	3	1	1	0	5
C	4	8	1	0	13
D	2	6	3	2	13
	16	20	10	4

7 — Page 41

	E	F	G	H	
A	2	1	4	4	11
B	1	9	4	7	21
C	5	3	0	0	8
D	5	6	6	8	25
	13	19	14	19

8 — Page 41

	E	F	G	H	
A	1	2	1	1	5
B	8	0	9	1	18
C	3	6	6	7	22
D	4	5	6	7	22
	16	13	22	16

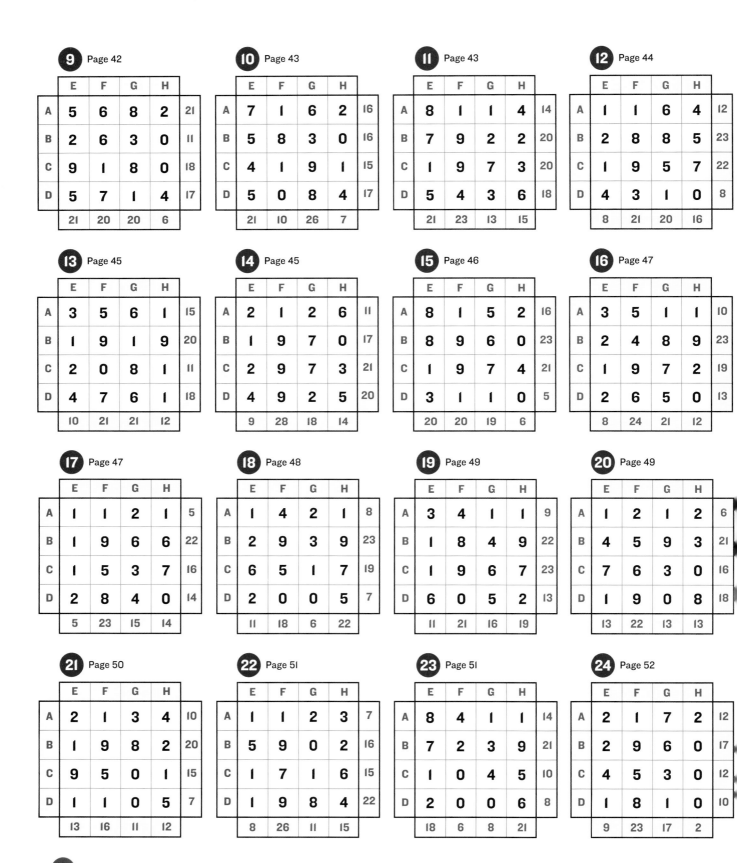

9 Page 42

	E	F	G	H	
A	5	6	8	2	21
B	2	6	3	0	11
C	9	1	8	0	18
D	5	7	1	4	17
	21	20	20	6	

10 Page 43

	E	F	G	H	
A	7	1	6	2	16
B	5	8	3	0	16
C	4	1	9	1	15
D	5	0	8	4	17
	21	10	26	7	

11 Page 43

	E	F	G	H	
A	8	1	1	4	14
B	7	9	2	2	20
C	1	9	7	3	20
D	5	4	3	6	18
	21	23	13	15	

12 Page 44

	E	F	G	H	
A	1	1	6	4	12
B	2	8	8	5	23
C	1	9	5	7	22
D	4	3	1	0	8
	8	21	20	16	

13 Page 45

	E	F	G	H	
A	3	5	6	1	15
B	1	9	1	9	20
C	2	0	8	1	11
D	4	7	6	1	18
	10	21	21	12	

14 Page 45

	E	F	G	H	
A	2	1	2	6	11
B	1	9	7	0	17
C	2	9	7	3	21
D	4	9	2	5	20
	9	28	18	14	

15 Page 46

	E	F	G	H	
A	8	1	5	2	16
B	8	9	6	0	23
C	1	9	7	4	21
D	3	1	1	0	5
	20	20	19	6	

16 Page 47

	E	F	G	H	
A	3	5	1	1	10
B	2	4	8	9	23
C	1	9	7	2	19
D	2	6	5	0	13
	8	24	21	12	

17 Page 47

	E	F	G	H	
A	1	1	2	1	5
B	1	9	6	6	22
C	1	5	3	7	16
D	2	8	4	0	14
	5	23	15	14	

18 Page 48

	E	F	G	H	
A	1	4	2	1	8
B	2	9	3	9	23
C	6	5	1	7	19
D	2	0	0	5	7
	11	18	6	22	

19 Page 49

	E	F	G	H	
A	3	4	1	1	9
B	1	8	4	9	22
C	1	9	6	7	23
D	6	0	5	2	13
	11	21	16	19	

20 Page 49

	E	F	G	H	
A	1	2	1	2	6
B	4	5	9	3	21
C	7	6	3	0	16
D	1	9	0	8	18
	13	22	13	13	

21 Page 50

	E	F	G	H	
A	2	1	3	4	10
B	1	9	8	2	20
C	9	5	0	1	15
D	1	1	0	5	7
	13	16	11	12	

22 Page 51

	E	F	G	H	
A	1	1	2	3	7
B	5	9	0	2	16
C	1	7	1	6	15
D	1	9	8	4	22
	8	26	11	15	

23 Page 51

	E	F	G	H	
A	8	4	1	1	14
B	7	2	3	9	21
C	1	0	4	5	10
D	2	0	0	6	8
	18	6	8	21	

24 Page 52

	E	F	G	H	
A	2	1	7	2	12
B	2	9	6	0	17
C	4	5	3	0	12
D	1	8	1	0	10
	9	23	17	2	

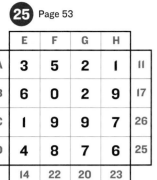

25 Page 53

	E	F	G	H	
A	3	5	2	1	11
B	6	0	2	9	17
C	1	9	9	7	26
D	4	8	7	6	25
	14	22	20	23	

26 Page 53

	E	F	G	H	
A	1	9	9	9	28
B	5	4	4	0	13
C	1	3	2	1	7
D	2	3	6	0	11
	9	19	21	10	

27 Page 54

	E	F	G	H	
A	8	5	6	1	20
B	1	9	7	9	26
C	2	3	4	7	16
D	1	1	0	9	11
	12	18	17	26	

28 Page 55

	E	F	G	H	
A	1	1	5	8	15
B	1	9	7	2	19
C	2	5	3	5	15
D	6	4	3	0	13
	10	19	18	15	

29 Page 55

	E	F	G	H	
A	7	4	1	4	16
B	5	0	9	4	18
C	1	9	6	8	24
D	7	8	2	3	20
	20	21	18	19	

30 Page 56

	E	F	G	H	
A	2	1	6	3	12
B	2	9	1	4	16
C	4	7	5	1	17
D	1	9	8	0	18
	9	26	20	8	

31 Page 57

	E	F	G	H	
A	3	6	1	2	12
B	2	1	2	0	5
C	1	9	5	0	15
D	7	6	2	8	23
	13	22	10	10	

32 Page 57

	E	F	G	H	
A	8	1	3	6	18
B	1	9	4	1	15
C	2	8	5	7	22
D	4	4	0	7	15
	15	22	12	21	

33 Page 58

	E	F	G	H	
A	9	1	7	4	21
B	5	9	2	0	16
C	8	3	3	6	20
D	1	9	7	1	18
	23	22	19	11	

34 Page 59

	E	F	G	H	
A	5	1	3	7	16
B	1	9	9	7	26
C	2	4	2	9	17
D	8	1	6	0	15
	16	15	20	23	

35 Page 59

	E	F	G	H	
A	4	1	1	0	6
B	1	8	6	3	18
C	1	9	7	4	21
D	5	6	2	7	20
	11	24	16	14	

36 Page 60

	E	F	G	H	
A	1	9	4	7	21
B	9	9	1	9	28
C	2	6	3	3	14
D	5	1	8	0	14
	17	25	16	19	

37 Page 61

	E	F	G	H	
A	4	1	3	6	14
B	1	9	7	3	20
C	1	8	2	0	11
D	9	8	5	1	23
	15	26	17	10	

38 Page 61

	E	F	G	H	
A	4	1	8	1	14
B	6	9	5	8	28
C	1	3	2	0	6
D	1	9	3	8	21
	12	22	18	17	

39 Page 62

	E	F	G	H	
A	7	1	1	6	15
B	1	9	8	3	21
C	4	5	4	0	13
D	2	6	8	4	20
	14	21	21	13	

40 Page 63

	E	F	G	H	
A	4	1	3	3	11
B	1	9	8	9	27
C	6	7	9	2	24
D	2	0	4	5	11
	13	17	24	19	

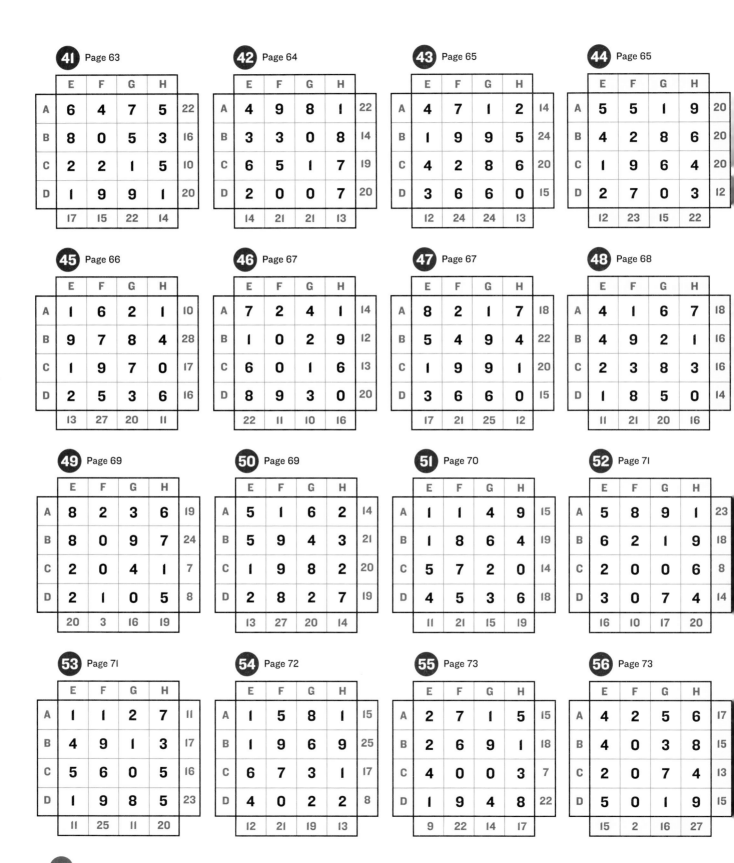

41 Page 63

	E	F	G	H	
A	6	4	7	5	22
B	8	0	5	3	16
C	2	2	1	5	10
D	1	9	9	1	20
	17	15	22	14	

42 Page 64

	E	F	G	H	
A	4	9	8	1	22
B	3	3	0	8	14
C	6	5	1	7	19
D	2	0	0	7	20
	14	21	21	13	

43 Page 65

	E	F	G	H	
A	4	7	1	2	14
B	1	9	9	5	24
C	4	2	8	6	20
D	3	6	6	0	15
	12	24	24	13	

44 Page 65

	E	F	G	H	
A	5	5	1	9	20
B	4	2	8	6	20
C	1	9	6	4	20
D	2	7	0	3	12
	12	23	15	22	

45 Page 66

	E	F	G	H	
A	1	6	2	1	10
B	9	7	8	4	28
C	1	9	7	0	17
D	2	5	3	6	16
	13	27	20	11	

46 Page 67

	E	F	G	H	
A	7	2	4	1	14
B	1	0	2	9	12
C	6	0	1	6	13
D	8	9	3	0	20
	22	11	10	16	

47 Page 67

	E	F	G	H	
A	8	2	1	7	18
B	5	4	9	4	22
C	1	9	9	1	20
D	3	6	6	0	15
	17	21	25	12	

48 Page 68

	E	F	G	H	
A	4	1	6	7	18
B	4	9	2	1	16
C	2	3	8	3	16
D	1	8	5	0	14
	11	21	20	16	

49 Page 69

	E	F	G	H	
A	8	2	3	6	19
B	8	0	9	7	24
C	2	0	4	1	7
D	2	1	0	5	8
	20	3	16	19	

50 Page 69

	E	F	G	H	
A	5	1	6	2	14
B	5	9	4	3	21
C	1	9	8	2	20
D	2	8	2	7	19
	13	27	20	14	

51 Page 70

	E	F	G	H	
A	1	1	4	9	15
B	1	8	6	4	19
C	5	7	2	0	14
D	4	5	3	6	18
	11	21	15	19	

52 Page 71

	E	F	G	H	
A	5	8	9	1	23
B	6	2	1	9	18
C	2	0	0	6	8
D	3	0	7	4	14
	16	10	17	20	

53 Page 71

	E	F	G	H	
A	1	1	2	7	11
B	4	9	1	3	17
C	5	6	0	5	16
D	1	9	8	5	23
	11	25	11	20	

54 Page 72

	E	F	G	H	
A	1	5	8	1	15
B	1	9	6	9	25
C	6	7	3	1	17
D	4	0	2	2	8
	12	21	19	13	

55 Page 73

	E	F	G	H	
A	2	7	1	5	15
B	2	6	9	1	18
C	4	0	0	3	7
D	1	9	4	8	22
	9	22	14	17	

56 Page 73

	E	F	G	H	
A	4	2	5	6	17
B	4	0	3	8	15
C	2	0	7	4	13
D	5	0	1	9	15
	15	2	16	27	

BIG TIME

Super Bowl   Pages 76–77

```
JAKE   PACT  OWL   BEN
OMAR   ASYE  RIO   APE
JERRYRICE    CNN   LET
ONLOW        LOSANGELES
     RCA  EFS  EST
AFC  ANY  FEAR  SNAP
NOON DUO  ASU   FOR
NEWYORKJETS    SULKY
  BARE  ATA   PSST
HOODS  DICKVERMEIL
ORY  OBE    EER   CAMP
TEST  RAMS  TRY   MPS
     ONO  CUP   YAP
JOEMONTANA     LOOKS
OWN  ICE  DANREEVES
HAY  SOD  AVIA  MART
NRA  ESS  YOKE  SLRS
```

Swimsuit Issue   Pages 78–79

```
BAR  BUM  KIM   BANKS
ACE  ERA  LOO   EMEER
IRELAND   UNO   TIEGS
TODOS  IAMS  MSN
     STAGG    BEYONCE
WALT  SATE  YDS   OAR
AFI  STN  RMN   ANNE
BAZAAR    INGEMAR
CRAWFORD  BRINKLEY
    RESULTS   LAYUPS
DENY  BEA   ALT   CEE
IVE  HOI  GAME  TIER
PATRICK    FIRPO
   ELS  DECA  IRANI
IRINA  HAL  BENITEZ
ODDER  URL  LET   ROZ
CASEY  RAE  ELO   ANO
```

March Madness   Pages 80–81

```
SODA  TAB  BYU   VAIL
ARAB  AMI  EDS   ISLS
MARCHMADNESS    LULU
ELK  MESSY    REL
   HOODS    MAR  LACES
AMOK      SEMIFINALS
FIRST  TATTOO  ONME
RNS  EVENS    REV
ONESEEDS   BIGDANCE
   INT   SEVEN  ORA
MARX  TRIPLE  ASSET
ELITEEIGHT    LEWS
LIBYA  MOE  CAROB
   FRI   REEVE  LGA
TAXI  SWEETSIXTEEN
UNLV  ION  AAA   WELT
BASE  NOD  SRS   ODDS
```

Sportscasters   Pages 82–83

```
RED   GET  DRAW   RRS
ACE   ANA  HULA  BEAT
HOWARDCOSELL    ANDI
   LYSOL     KOREAN
CIDE    DICKENBERG
FLORIDA   DEERE
LEG  RUSSELL   SKIPS
   COSTAS     WAVE
JIMMCKAY   JIMNANTZ
ISAO       BUTTON
BRENT  BOITANO   RIM
   ATOLL   TSKTSKS
ALMICHAELS     ATEN
TOUCHE     HAGEN
ETTA  KEITHJACKSON
ATTN  IDLE   ASH  USE
MSS   DUKE  RHO  BUD
```

The Masters   Pages 84–85

```
PAM  AAS  ETHS  RAES
GAP  IST  SHOW  ERMA
AUGUSTA   SEGA   SEMI
   CLINT   NATIONAL
BUTLERCABIN    GRASS
ASIA   ERA    GOT
GAL  WAS  LIMA   NAE
   MAR  TIGERWOODS
DISTANCE   ONCOURSE
AMENCORNER     IRT
BAT    LOTT  TAN  OUR
   AND   TWO   NATE
SMITH  GREENJACKET
NICKLAUS   SIENA
ONEI  SEVE  GEORGIA
REIN  TSPS  HRS   OAR
TONS  ITSA  TSE   ONT
```

Sports Clichés   Pages 86–87

```
WHOS  ASK   USS   PIC
HACK  DIE   SHUT  LOU
ASTI  ALP   HOLESOUT
THATSGOTTAHURT
   ORE  ARN     UFOS
   ITWASATEAMEFFORT
ASA   VIA   AXE   RBS
DOME  MATT  NCAA
DFENCE      ERUPTS
   TOES  GAIL  SOHO
PRY  MTS  EBB    LAX
THERESNOTOMORROW
AERO    REV   PDA
   ONEGAMEATATIME
GOLFCART   PSI  IDOL
ASP  ATIE  ATO  NELL
BUS  RST   RAN  GATE
```

No. 1 Draft Picks   Pages 88–89

```
REC   ESP  SPAS  BRAD
ERA   ART  CURT  ROSE
NIGERIA    ONCE  ATTA
ONEAL    SOUTHERNCAL
    RED  TRAILED
SOP   EAT  EEN   OLE
KWAMEBROWN    REINED
ANTONIO   HOD   RBIS
    EOS  STEVE  FAO
CARR   EON  ALABAMA
ERNEST   PITTSBURGH
LEO  LIT  AHA   DBS
   TARHEEL    TIM
QUARTERBACK    POSSE
USNA  MOBS  YAOMING
ITUP  ANET  LID   MIO
TATS  NEDS  ELS   STS
```

Sports Movies   Pages 90–91

```
HRS   KOBE  PAN   FIRE
EEL   ALOT  GIA   ISON
LEATHERHEADS    FUND
IFYOU   GIL    TUT
    NNE  CADDYSHACK
BIGEAST   III   ASNAP
ASA   THUNDER    YRS
TATUM  ONE    COLT
HOOSIERS   SLAPSHOT
   REAL    OUI  QUIPS
ARA   YANKEES   NIA
RADIO  SOS  SLUGGER
THENATURAL   OSE
   PRE   NAT  ATALL
JOEL  BREAKINGAWAY
AREA  OAT  ERIE  ERN
MARY  WES  REPS  DAN
```

World Series   Pages 92–93

```
SPAR  ALPS  VET   CEY
PASO  SEAU  IRE   UKE
ATHLETICS   PIRATES
   LVI   EPA   KILO
RACIER   END   OFME
ELLEN  SANDYKOUFAX
HAI  IFOLD  EAR  STP
AMMO  ALES   LEA
BOBBYCOX   PHILLIES
   JAI   ARUN  ACRE
ARM  DNA  LOBES  ARA
CHICAGOCUBS    AKRON
HERO    KIM  OWNERS
   ARIZ  AIM  CII
JACKSON  NIGHTGAME
OWL  UNI  UNTO  HALL
EEE  PEP  MESA  TABS
```

College Mascots   Pages 94–95

```
FILM  FLY  MET   NORM
ATOE  LEE  ODO   EFOR
BULLDOGS   DIRTBAGS
   PATIO   SETTER
    ORG  HRS   NAMES
TIGER  RYAN    SOSO
EVAN   EAR   HOKIES
RAZORBACKS    ONA
INE   AUTH  TALC  TOM
   CTR  THUNDERING
PLAYER   ONO   RVER
BANC    PUTT  FROGS
APOLO  AIS  ESL
   ORANGE    LEADS
RAINBOWS   BLUEHENS
ACRE  NAT  BIG  ELOI
MESS  ERY  QBS  MAWR
```

UNDER REVIEW

Items that have been altered, starting from the left side of the photos:

Page 98–99
The Long Run
1. Wells's uniform name changed to *Weels* 2. Wells's socks made all red 3. Ball moved from ground to Fitzgerald's hands 4. Harrison's number on jersey flipped 5. White stripe added on referee's sock 6. Referee's right wristband is removed 7. No. 25's shoulder pads tucked in 8. The black on Fitzgerald's shoes now red

Page 100–01
Track Meat
1. Helmet on Rockies player leaning against fence now a cap 2. The No. 1 sausage's eyelids are altered 3. Yellow button removed from No. 1's outfit 4. Catcher's shin guard now all black 5. Number of brown lines on No. 5's shirt reduced from two to one 6. No. 2's ear is removed 7. Red and purple stripes on No. 2's shirt are reversed 8. No. 3's eyebrows are removed 9. Lettering on back of staffer's red shirt removed 10. Shirt color of fan by foul pole is changed from yellow to blue

Page 102–03
Into the Blue
1. Yellow wristband on blue arm is removed 2. Unpainted face (toward top, behind arm) is now painted 3. White spot on blue face, two fans to the right, is gone 4. Glasses on mustached man at table removed 5. Word *Carolina* on uniform changed to *Carilina* 6. Player's mouth has been closed 7. Armband added on player's left arm 8. Letter *D* on fan's chest becomes a *U* 8. Added fan head, three heads up from ball 9. Woman's face at table is painted

Page 104–05
Passing Lanes
1. Red shoe near bottom left becomes blue 2. Yellow lane marker now white 3. White headband now blue 4. Blue baton now white 5. Necklace from runner near center removed 6. Emblem on AZ's jersey removed 7. Foot shadow near AZ removed 8. BA's pant leg made all blue 9. BD's tag changed to BB 10. AR's baton missing

Page 106–07
Over and Out
1. Fan removed from right of blonde woman at top left 2. Player's sleeve lengthened 3. Glove of fan in striped shirt removed 4. Fan's head, two spots to right, has been replaced with that of Yankees pitcher Joba Chamberlain 5. Ball moved to the right 6. Panels in fencing flipped 7. Lettering removed from white security shirt 8. Cup with red straw in stands now filled with beer 9. Yankee fan has hair thickened and moustache added

Page 108–09
Prepare for Landing
1. Piece removed from harness on horse's nose 2. Piece removed from reins in rider's right hand 3. Band on left hand changed 4. Top strap on boot removed 5. Bamboo piece removed from left section of obstacle 6. Purple item on shelf in left obstacle section removed 7. Horse's tail shortened 8. White mark on horse's rear leg minimized 9. Black band removed from wood bundle at bottom right of obstacle 10. Knot added to wood on top beam of obstacle.

Page 110–11
High and Mighty
1. Player waiting to enter at scorer's table removed 2. Team banners on back left wall are flipped 3. Word *Xavier* on No. 24's uniform changed to *Xeviar*. 4. Ball moved higher on backboard 5. Left defender's kneeband removed 6. Bud Light sign changed to Budweiser 7. Numbers on shot clock have changed. 8. Right defender's right arm removed 9. Right defender's socks are lowered 10. Retired uniforms at upper right changed from black to white

Page 112–13
A Posing Force
1. Shin guard stripe added on front left player 2. Skate blade removed on second reclining player from left 3. Facial hair removed from player near back row with cap turned around 4. Letter *S* removed from ice 5. Stanley Cup broadened at top of base 6. Two players removed from back row, middle, and replaced with fan in white shirt 7. Trio of fans shifted one row to right 8. Fan's gray hoodie changed to Red Wings jersey 9. Red Wings logo reversed on jersey in front row, far right 10. Blue necktie changed to red

Page 114–15
Prime Interest
1. Sunglasses added to staffer 2. Microphone arm added 3. Red sleeve in foreground changed to blue 4. Stripe added on Sanders's right sleeve 5. Sanders's left thumb removed 6. Sanders's visor bill removed 7. Microphone pole color changed to black 8. Microphone cable shape altered

Page 116–17
Running Out of Water
1. Splash made larger in front of leftmost swimmer 2. Arm behind that swimmer in the background flipped 3. Red buoy added by water's far edge 4. Colors changed on building in background 5. Boat flags reversed 6. Ertel's cap changed 7. Haskins's Speedo logo reversed 8. Leg of red-suited swimmer now covered

Page 118–19
Big Easy Reading
1. Fan in light yellow shirt on left goes from making "No. 1" gesture to "Hook 'em Horns" sign 2. No. 18 fan's tassels now all purple 3. Word *laissez* on sign changed to *leissez* 4. Piping on gray shirt changed from yellow to purple 5. In paper of woman in yellow shirt, headline altered to read *Ohio State Turns Back LSU* 6. Fan's camera toward top right removed 7. White cap changed to purple 8. LSU button changed 9. No. 15 in bottom right newspaper photo becomes No. 16

Page 120–121
Legging It Out
1. Letter *S* on Syracuse shorts made white 2. Cornell player's stick end narrowed 3. TX lettering on pad removed 4. Color of Syracuse player's arm gear made red 5. Bar added to Cornell player's face mask 6. Red part of Cornell player's glove made white 7. STX lettering on Syracuse player's glove changed to *STY* 8. Ball moved to the right 9. Background player number becomes double digits 10. Nike swoosh on Cornell player's heel reversed

Page 122–23
Boom Time
1. Fan in red shirt on the far left now holding a camera 2. Beer of top-row fan in gray shirt removed 3. Light stand added in front row, above Pavano 4. Dirt removed from cleat cleaner on mound 5. Umpire's right knee

removed **6**. Catcher's left shoulder pad added **7**. McGwire given a second shin guard **8**. Arms switched on fan in white T-shirt at far right

Page 124–25
Mogul Mayhem
I. Hat added to official at far left **2**. Shades of green reversed in signage at top of hill **3**. Dot removed from the *i* in Torino **4**. Light above yellow arc removed **5**. Height of mogul to left of the skier increased **6**. Ski positions flipped—top now on bottom **7**. Torino 2006 lettering added to snow at bottom **8**. TV equipment cable removed

Page 126–27
Quick Change Artists
I. Blue hose added to left of car **2**. Red bumper of car at top now yellow **3**. Car number changed from 48 to 40 **4**. Chevy logo flipped on front of hood **5**. The word *Lowe's* flipped on leg of crew member to right of car **6**. Radio added to same crew member **7**. Man in red-white-and-blue helmet removed **8**. Tire added at top right

Page 128–29
The Green Party
I. Flag on Donald Driver's helmet flipped **2**. Red cap now green, on fan directly above Driver **3**. Beer bottle added, above "First Game" sign **4**. Lettering on foam stick above Jennings changed **5**. Jennings's uniform name becomes *Jenninings* **6**. Ring finger on Jennings's glove changed from white to black **7**. Glasses of fan over Lee's shoulder now sunglasses **8**. Cup in black gloved hand to right of Lee removed **9**. Barrier height raised

Page 130–31
Dish Network
I. Number and team changed in team-foul counter on arena rim **2**. Ariza's shoelace color changed from black to purple **3**. *Playoffs* sign at midlevel becomes *Lakers* sign **4**. Ball rotated **5**. Trio of courtside fans to left of No. 96 changed **6**. Net made to hang straight **7**. No. 96 on uniform changed to 66 **8**. Logo on Bryant's shorts flipped **9**. No. 0's facial hair removed

Page 132–33
Crash Scene
I. Prince Fielder's left foot removed **2**. Nike swoosh on Koskie's right foot removed **3**. Home plate reversed **4**. Koskie's arm angle

changed **5**. Catcher's left leg angle changed **6**. Pointing gesture in shadow made into fist **7**. Niekro's sleeve logo removed **8**. Catcher's glove flipped

Page 134–35
Golden Moment
I. Railing at far left removed **2**. Purple camera strap removed, on man wearing white T-shirt with red piping, toward bottom **3**. Woman's hair part reversed, toward top left **4**. Lettering on photo vest at bottom removed **5**. Watch changed on photographer touching woman's shoulder **6** White dot removed in Beijing T-shirt logo of man behind Debbie Phelps **7**. Camera in fan's hand removed, to right of Debbie Phelps **8**. Color of camera near bottom goes from metallic to black **9**. Bald spot on gray-haired photograper toward bottom right covered up **10**. Some stripes removed on red shirt of fan at far right

FRONT COVER

(left to right, top to bottom) John G. Zimmerman, Simon Bruty, John Biever, Simon Bruty, Tony Triolo, Simon Bruty, Damian Strohmeyer, Heinz Kluetmeier, Al Tielemans, John Biever

CONTENTS

3 (clockwise from left) Bob Martin, John W. McDonough, Raphael Mazzucco, John Biever

STARTERS

4 (clockwise from left) Robert Beck, Simon Bruty, Tony Triolo; 5 (clockwise from left), Damian Strohmeyer (2), Robert Beck; 6 Robert Beck; 7 Robert Beck; 8 Heinz Kluetmeier; 9 Chuck Solomon; 10 David E. Klutho; 11 David E. Klutho; 12 John W. McDonough; 13 Walter Iooss Jr.; 14 Bob Martin; 15 Bob Martin; 16 Simon Bruty; 17 Simon Bruty; 18 Robert Beck; 19 Robert Beck; 20 Damian Strohmeyer; 21 Manny Millan; 22 Tony Triolo; 23 Manny Millan; 24 Damian Strohmeyer; 25 John Biever; 26 Damian Strohmeyer; 27 Bob Rosato; 28 Simon Bruty; 29 Bob Martin; 30 John Biever; 31 John Biever; 32 John Biever; 33 Heinz Kluetmeier

CROSS STATS

34 (from left) Heinz Kluetmeier, Manny Millan; 35 (from left) John W. McDonough, Walter Iooss Jr.; 36 Walter Iooss Jr.; 37 (from top) Bob Martin, John Biever; 38 (from top) John Biever, Walter Iooss Jr.; 39 (from top) John Iacono, John W. McDonough; 40 (from top) Neil Leifer, John W. McDonough; 41 (from top) Simon Bruty, Heinz Kluetmeier; 42 (from top) Andy Hayt, Robert Beck; 43 (from top) Manny Millan, John Iacono; 44 (from top) Heinz Kluetmeier, John Iacono; 45 (from top) Heinz Kluetmeier, Walter Iooss Jr.; 46 Tony Triolo, John W. McDonough; 47 (from top) John Biever, Manny Millan; 48 (from top) John Biever, Tony Triolo; 49 (from top) Heinz Kluetmeier, John W. McDonough; 50 Walter Iooss Jr. (2); 51 (from top) Bill Frakes, John Biever; 52 (from top) Al Tielemans, Manny Millan; 53 (from top) John G. Zimmerman, Simon Bruty; 54 (from top) John Iacono, Robert Beck; 55 (from top) Walter Iooss Jr., David E. Klutho; 56 John Iacono (2); 57 (from top) Heinz Kluetmeier, Bill Frakes; 58 (from top) Manny Millan, Al Tielemans; 59 (from top) Walter Iooss Jr., James Drake; 60 (from top) Tony Triolo, Bob Rosato; 61 (from top) Heinz Kluetmeier, Andy Hayt; 62 (from top) Walter Iooss Jr., Herb Scharfman; 63 (from top) Andy Hayt, Neil Leifer; 64 (from top) Walter Iooss Jr., Damian Strohmeyer; 65 (from top) Manny Millan, Andy Hayt; 66 (from top) Heinz Kluetmeier (2); 67 (from top) Peter Read Miller, Bill Frakes; 68 (from top) David E. Klutho, John Biever; 69 (from top) Heinz Kluetmeier, Robert Beck; 70 (from top) Heinz Kluetmeier, Walter Iooss Jr.; 71 (from top) John W. McDonough, Ronald C. Modra; 72 (from top) John W. McDonough, Neil Leifer; 73 (from top) John Iacono, Bob Rosato

BIG TIME

74 (clockwise from left) John W. McDonough, Bob Rosato, Lane Stewart; 75 (clockwise from left) Walter Iooss Jr., Al Tielemans, Heinz Kluetmeier; 76 (from left) Al Tielemans, Andy Hayt; 78 (from left) Walter Iooss Jr., Raphael Mazzucco; 80 (from left) Carl Skalak, Bob Rosato; 82 (from left) Lane Stewart, Carl Iwasaki; 84 (from left) Heinz Kluetmeier, John Iacono; 86 (from left) John Biever, Bill Frakes; 88 (from left) Manny Millan, Walter Iooss Jr.; 90 (from left) 20th Century Fox Film Corp./Everett Collection, Warner Bros./Everett Collection; 92 Walter Iooss Jr.; 94 (from left) John W. McDonough, John Biever

UNDER REVIEW

96–97 Bill Frakes, John Biever (Steelers uniform), Heinz Kluetmeier (mustache); 98–99 John Biever; 100–101 John Biever; 102–103 Bob Rosato; 104–105 Heinz Kluetmeier; 106–107 John Biever, Chuck Solomon (head); 108–109 Bob Martin; 110–111 Al Tielemans; 112–113 David E. Klutho; 114–115 John Iacono; 116–117 Bob Martin; 118–119 Damian Strohmeyer; 120–121 Bill Frakes; 122–123 David E. Klutho; 124–125 Bob Martin; 126–127 David E. Klutho; 128–129 John Biever; 130–131 John W. McDonough; 132–133 John Biever; 134–135 John W. McDonough

BACK COVER

(left to right, top to bottom) John W. McDonough, Bob Rosato, John G. Zimmerman, John Iacono (2), Manny Millan, Robert Beck, John Biever, Heinz Kluetmeier, Manny Millan

EDITOR Bill Syken **ART DIRECTOR** Patrick Merrell **PHOTO EDITOR** Jennifer R. Grad **CROSSWORDS** Patrick Merrell **CROSS STATS** Mike Baranack **PICTURE PUZZLES** Dan Larkin, Geoff Michaud, Robert M. Thompson **COPY EDITOR** Kevin Kerr **DESIGNER** Josh Denkin **WRITER** Elizabeth McGarr **REPORTER** Rebecca Shore **SPECIAL THANKS TO** Steven Hoffman, Stefanie Kaufman, Gabe Miller, Suzanne Noli, Cristina Scalet, Stephen Skalocky and Sports Illustrated Group Editor Terry McDonell

Time Inc. Home Entertainment **PUBLISHER** Richard Fraiman **GENERAL MANAGER** Steven Sandonato **EXECUTIVE DIRECTOR, MARKETING SERVICES** Carol Pittard **DIRECTOR, RETAIL & SPECIAL SALES** Tom Mifsud **DIRECTOR, NEW PRODUCT DEVELOPMENT** Peter Harper **ASSISTANT DIRECTOR, BOOKAZINE MARKETING** Laura Adam **ASSISTANT PUBLISHING DIRECTOR, BRAND MARKETING** Joy Butts **ASSOCIATE COUNSEL** Helen Wan **BRAND & LICENSING MANAGER** Alexandra Bliss **DESIGN & PREPRESS MANAGER** Anne-Michelle Gallero **BOOK PRODUCTION MANAGER** Susan Chodakiewicz **ASSOCIATE BRAND MANAGER** Allison Parker **SPECIAL THANKS TO** Christine Austin, Glenn Buonocore, Jim Childs, Rose Cirrincione, Jacqueline Fitzgerald, Lauren Hall, Jennifer Jacobs, Suzanne Janso, Brynn Joyce, Mona Li, Robert Marasco, Amy Migliaccio, Brooke Reger, Dave Rozzelle, Ilene Schreider, Adriana Tierno, Alex Voznesenskiy and Sydney Webber